The vicar of Lansdowne; or country quarters. In two volumes. By Regina Maria Roche. ... Second edition. Volume 1 of 2

Regina Maria Roche

ECCO
PRINT EDITIONS

Gale ECCO Print Editions

Relive history with *Eighteenth Century Collections Online*, now available in print for the independent historian and collector. This series includes the most significant English-language and foreign-language works printed in Great Britain during the eighteenth century, and is organized in seven different subject areas including literature and language; medicine, science, and technology; and religion and philosophy. The collection also includes thousands of important works from the Americas.

The eighteenth century has been called "The Age of Enlightenment." It was a period of rapid advance in print culture and publishing, in world exploration, and in the rapid growth of science and technology – all of which had a profound impact on the political and cultural landscape. At the end of the century the American Revolution, French Revolution and Industrial Revolution, perhaps three of the most significant events in modern history, set in motion developments that eventually dominated world political, economic, and social life.

In a groundbreaking effort, Gale initiated a revolution of its own: digitization of epic proportions to preserve these invaluable works in the largest online archive of its kind. Contributions from major world libraries constitute over 175,000 original printed works. Scanned images of the actual pages, rather than transcriptions, recreate the works *as they first appeared.*

Now for the first time, these high-quality digital scans of original works are available via print-on-demand, making them readily accessible to libraries, students, independent scholars, and readers of all ages.

For our initial release we have created seven robust collections to form one the world's most comprehensive catalogs of 18th century works.

Initial Gale ECCO Print Editions collections include:

History and Geography
Rich in titles on English life and social history, this collection spans the world as it was known to eighteenth-century historians and explorers. Titles include a wealth of travel accounts and diaries, histories of nations from throughout the world, and maps and charts of a world that was still being discovered. Students of the War of American Independence will find fascinating accounts from the British side of conflict.

Social Science

Delve into what it was like to live during the eighteenth century by reading the first-hand accounts of everyday people, including city dwellers and farmers, businessmen and bankers, artisans and merchants, artists and their patrons, politicians and their constituents. Original texts make the American, French, and Industrial revolutions vividly contemporary.

Medicine, Science and Technology

Medical theory and practice of the 1700s developed rapidly, as is evidenced by the extensive collection, which includes descriptions of diseases, their conditions, and treatments. Books on science and technology, agriculture, military technology, natural philosophy, even cookbooks, are all contained here.

Literature and Language

Western literary study flows out of eighteenth-century works by Alexander Pope, Daniel Defoe, Henry Fielding, Frances Burney, Denis Diderot, Johann Gottfried Herder, Johann Wolfgang von Goethe, and others. Experience the birth of the modern novel, or compare the development of language using dictionaries and grammar discourses.

Religion and Philosophy

The Age of Enlightenment profoundly enriched religious and philosophical understanding and continues to influence present-day thinking. Works collected here include masterpieces by David Hume, Immanuel Kant, and Jean-Jacques Rousseau, as well as religious sermons and moral debates on the issues of the day, such as the slave trade. The Age of Reason saw conflict between Protestantism and Catholicism transformed into one between faith and logic -- a debate that continues in the twenty-first century.

Law and Reference

This collection reveals the history of English common law and Empire law in a vastly changing world of British expansion. Dominating the legal field is the *Commentaries of the Law of England* by Sir William Blackstone, which first appeared in 1765. Reference works such as almanacs and catalogues continue to educate us by revealing the day-to-day workings of society.

Fine Arts

The eighteenth-century fascination with Greek and Roman antiquity followed the systematic excavation of the ruins at Pompeii and Herculaneum in southern Italy; and after 1750 a neoclassical style dominated all artistic fields. The titles here trace developments in mostly English-language works on painting, sculpture, architecture, music, theater, and other disciplines. Instructional works on musical instruments, catalogs of art objects, comic operas, and more are also included.

The BiblioLife Network

This project was made possible in part by the BiblioLife Network (BLN), a project aimed at addressing some of the huge challenges facing book preservationists around the world. The BLN includes libraries, library networks, archives, subject matter experts, online communities and library service providers. We believe every book ever published should be available as a high-quality print reproduction; printed on-demand anywhere in the world. This insures the ongoing accessibility of the content and helps generate sustainable revenue for the libraries and organizations that work to preserve these important materials.

The following book is in the "public domain" and represents an authentic reproduction of the text as printed by the original publisher. While we have attempted to accurately maintain the integrity of the original work, there are sometimes problems with the original work or the micro-film from which the books were digitized. This can result in minor errors in reproduction. Possible imperfections include missing and blurred pages, poor pictures, markings and other reproduction issues beyond our control. Because this work is culturally important, we have made it available as part of our commitment to protecting, preserving, and promoting the world's literature.

GUIDE TO FOLD-OUTS MAPS and OVERSIZED IMAGES

The book you are reading was digitized from microfilm captured over the past thirty to forty years. Years after the creation of the original microfilm, the book was converted to digital files and made available in an online database.

In an online database, page images do not need to conform to the size restrictions found in a printed book. When converting these images back into a printed bound book, the page sizes are standardized in ways that maintain the detail of the original. For large images, such as fold-out maps, the original page image is split into two or more pages

Guidelines used to determine how to split the page image follows:

• Some images are split vertically; large images require vertical and horizontal splits.
• For horizontal splits, the content is split left to right.
• For vertical splits, the content is split from top to bottom.
• For both vertical and horizontal splits, the image is processed from top left to bottom right.

THE

VICAR OF LANSDOWNE.

A TALE.

LANE, MINERVA-PRESS, LEADENHALL-STREET.

THE

VICAR OF LANSDOWNE;

OR

COUNTRY QUARTERS.

IN TWO VOLUMES.

BY

REGINA MARIA ROCHE.

AUTHOR OF

The Children of the Abbey, Maid of the Hamlet, Clermont, &c

" Ye fmiling band
" Of youths and virgins, who thro' all the maze
" Of young defire with rival fteps purfue
" The charm of beauty, if the pleafing toil
" Can yield a moment's refpite, hither turn
" Your *favourable* ear."

AKENSIDE.

VOL. I.

Second Edition.

LONDON:

PRINTED AT THE

Minerva Press,

FOR WILLIAM LANE, LEADENHALL-STREET.

1800.

DEDICATION.

THE Author of the following Work gladly embraces the present opportunity of returning her most grateful acknowledgments to the Public, for the high favour and patronage it has already experienced from them;

for

for which she is convinced she is more indebted to their candour and liberality than to any intrinsic merit it possesses. She hopes, by having attentively revised and corrected it, she may have rendered it more worthy their notice; and with humility and gratitude dedicates it to them.

London, Aug. 13, 1800.

ADDRESS.

I INVOKE not you, ye Tuneful Nine, who fit enthroned on Mount Parnaſſus; an invocation to the Muſes I reſerve for a more important occaſion, when ſublimity may be eſſential to the dignity of my theme, or wit be required to gild my pages with the brightneſs of its-beams.

To you, Oh ye critics! I addreſs my fervent prayer; and I implore you to

diſregard

difregard this humble TALE. The amufement of a few folitary hours cannot be worthy of your high attention. Unftudied, unornamented as it is, it may, perhaps, beguile fome tedious interval, if your cenfures do not cruelly crufh the flattering hope, and ftifle my poor bantling on its firft ftruggles into life. Permit it, I entreat you, to pafs by in unheeded infignificance, and referve your fagacious animadverfions for thofe ftupendous works that, like the Pyramids of Egypt, rife fucceffively above each other, and provoke, by their pretenfions to fame, an enquiry into the nature of their ftructure, and the bafis of their elevation.

THE
VICAR
OF
LANSDOWNE.

CHAP. I.

THE PARADE.

A DETACHMENT of a regiment of foot was quartered at Lansdowne, a beautiful village, at a considerable distance from the metropolis. The Officers belonging to it were convivially assembled in "the best inn's best room;" and their conversation turning upon the subject of country quarters, a general declamation prevailed againſt the intolerable hardſhips they impoſed. One vowed that he had been almoſt deſtroyed at Earlswood, by ſpending an evening with the Exciſeman's wife. Another ſwore that he ſhould never recover from the effects of his viſit to the Parſon's lady; her loquacity was as endleſs as her huſband's homilies, her hoſpitality more fatal than a city feaſt, and her affectation worſe than the barbariſm of an *Eſquimaux belle*.

"Batter me from a fortreſs," cried a third, "but I would ſooner ſuffer a ten weeks ſiege, than ſit two hours with what are called your country miſſes, their confound- ing clack aſſaſſinates my ears more inſuffer- ably than a cannonading; and I would ſooner fly from their overſtrained civilities than I ſhould from a troop of Otaheiteans, or the clutches of an enraged wild Iriſhman."

"Yet

"Yet rural innocence," obferved a fourth, " has ever been a favourite fubject of the poet's pen."

" Rural innocence!" anfwered one of them, " pri'thee, where does it now exift? Arcadia, my dear fellow, no longer flourifhes but in the warm regions of fancy and imagination, and fhould we fearch for the reality of that chafte and lovely fimplicity which the paftoral poets have defcribed, the pleafing portrait would vanifh from our view, and convince us that they have only given " to airy nothing a local habitation and a name." Every gale wafts the folly and caprice of the metropolis to its neighbouring fhades; the infection is fpread from place to place by the natural vanity of the fex; and however it may decreafe by tranfmiffion, the deftructive poifon has, in fome degree, penetrated the moft fequeftered receffes of the island. If country miſſes, indeed, would confine themſelves to their proper ſphere, they might be bearable; but when an awkward, overgrown, robuſt hoyden, deſigned by nature for the offices of the dairy, talks of the pleaſures of a town life, accuſes papa of cruelty in confining her to woods unconſcious of her charms, cries, with a ſide-glance at the glaſs, ' what a conſpicuous place is the boxes to diſplay a fine figure!' and, falling into the moſt ridiculous attitudes, practiſes airs of affectation, the meaning of which ſhe is too ignorant to comprehend, and too taſteleſs to render elegant, ſhe appears like an ill-made garment, which only expoſes, in a more prepoſterous manner, every natural defect."

" May I be ſhot," exclaimed a young Enſign, " if I don't conſider ſuch beings like natural curioſities. I once entertained

a deſign

a defign to fend a group of them, as a prefent, to my uncle, who, you know, is a man of *virtù*; they would have made an admirable addition to petrified mufcles, toads, fcorpions, and preferved cameleons."

While this converfation was paffing in the room,-two young Officers, who were lounging out from one of the windows, uttered the exclamation, " charming!" with fuch a tone of emphafis that it attracted the attention of the difputants, and terminated a difcourfe which would foon have proved that a country nymph, pretending to elegance, is one of the greateft monfters in the arcana of nature, and that *ennui* and caprice, in her mouth, are juft as intolerable as domeftic blifs, or rational joys, from the lips of a modern fine lady.

Directly oppofite to this window was a little walk, regularly planted with two rows of elms, which the villagers called the mall, and the Officers the parade. To this walk the young ladies of the village conftantly reforted every evening; and employed all the artillery of drefs and beauty, to befiege the hearts of their attendant fwains; and on this parade as proud a pleafure was felt in difplaying the humble finery of rural life, as was ever experienced by the rival *belles* and *beaux* of the metropolis, robed in all the fplendour of a birth-day ball, or midnight mafquerade.

Among the fair group, who now preffed this verdant walk, were two laffes, whofe fuperior charms plainly evinced that nature fometimes beftows her gifts on the inhabitants of woods and waterfalls. The eyes of one of them, every now and then, flily glanced toward the window from which the Officers were lounging, attracted, we prefume, by

the

the number of cockades, and the *jeu d'esprit* so inseparable from the military character.

The Officers immediately deserted the room, and, to use a military phrase, repaired directly to the scene of action.

Had we the powers of those renowned geniuses who have so inimitably described the combats of the sexes, we might attempt to relate the little stratagems, or paint the smiling loves and graces, which were exhibited to attract the admiration of these military heroes. But suffice it to say with Villars in the Belle's Stratagem, that they were soon convinced they had entered on an enterprise almost as dangerous as an encounter with Paul Jones, or a midnight march to Omai.

It was drawing towards that romantic hour when the moon, silvering the firmament, invites those pensive souls who talk of love,

and

and feel or create imaginary woes, to come forth and vent their forrows in cadence with the wild notes of Philomel, when the nymphs, whofe native charms had extorted the flattering exclamation from the. Officers, quitted the parade, but they left it not unattended. The fprightly levity of one of them had conjured up the very fpirit of gallantry; and two of the Officers, whofe fuperior manners marked their higher origin, prefumed to trace their footfteps. A fignificant fqueeze, which one of the ladies was obferved to give to the arm of her fair companion, accompanied with a certain motion of the head, indicated no difapprobation of their being the objects of the purfuit, but there was fomething in the *tout enfemble* of their demeanour, that infpired refpect and veneration, and protected them from the rudenefs of an abrupt addrefs. The Officers

filently

filently followed their fair f g tive, anxioufly wifhing that the appearance of fome of thofe fatyrs, who were the moleftation of the nymphs of old, would afford them an opportunity of offering their affiftance and protection.

Chance, in a laughing mood, at length indulged their wifhes, but by the intervention of an animal far more harmlefs than an ancient fatyr.

A white cow fuddenly ftarted forward from her entanglement among the branches of an adjacent copfe, and the fair ones, of courfe, as fuddenly ftarted back. One of them, with the prettieft fcream imaginable, vowed fhe was frightened out of her life. Life, however, never more fkilfully performed its functions than at this moment: it darted in radiance from her eyes, and

B 5 mantled

mantled her cheeks with the crimfon glow
of health, pleafure, and vivacity.

Gallantry, it is faid, never appears in
fo irrefiftible a form as when clothed *à
la militaire*, and our heroes were by no
means ignorant of that graceful eafe, that
infinuating addrefs, that enchanting etiquette,
which diftinguifh men of elegance from
thofe who have never facrificed to the graces.

On hearing the fcream of invitation, they
immediately flew forward to offer their fervices upon fo alarming an event; but the
cow had marched quietly away, and refufed
to give them the opportunity, an animal of
the fame kind once gave to the Earl of
Warwick, of enrolling their courage in the
annals of renown.

The opportunity, however, of gratifying
their more immediate wifhes was not to be
neglected; they expreffed a well-feigned
concern for the fright this incident had occafioned,

sioned, represented the dangers to which ladies who walk unprotected are continually exposed, and concluded by ardently requesting permission to become their escort.

The intimidated fair one, in trembling recovery from the effects of her alarm, with a soft but inarticulate voice, thanked them for their politeness, but neither wholly indulged, nor quite repressed the offer of protection. She half smiled, half frowned; but her frowns, like mists before the sun, soon vanished, and in defiance of the rebuking countenance of her companion, she at length permitted them to walk by her side. Whether this permission was strictly consistent with female propriety, we shall leave to the prudes to determine. It must be confessed that she had frequently trod the same path at a much later hour, without the smallest apprehension, allowance, however,

B 6   ought

ought to be made for the agitation her fright
had occafioned.

Having adopted the means of fafety, her
ideas of danger foon vanifhed, and fhe
giggled, laughed, and rattled away, with
all the vivacity which good fpirits and unexpected pleafure naturally infpire; while
the impropriety of this levity feemed to be
filently cenfured by the grave deportment
of her companion. The converfation, highly
pleafing as it was to the fpeakers, might not
prove quite fo delectable to our readers, we
fhall therefore forbear to defcribe it, and
only remark, that it confifted, as is ufual
upon fuch occafions, of fine compliments,
expreffions of happinefs, anfwers of courfe,
&c. &c. &c.

The party at length arrived within fight of
a neat houfe, when the lively little chatterer,
with a faucy archnefs which implied a con-

fcicufnefs

fcioufnefs of the favour fhe had conferred, returned her protectors thanks for their civility, and her companion acknowledging her gratitude by a curtfy, they both tripped away, leaving the Officers to obferve their route in filent admiration, until the door of the houfe enclofed them from their view.

Captain Melford, for that was the name of one of thefe heroes. on their return to country quarters, expreffed his fentiments of the character of his lively favourite in the higheft ftrains of panegyric. " The *naiveté* of that girl," faid he, " will do more execution in lefs time, by the open, artlefs, unaffected fprightlinefs of her manner, than women of three times her beauty. While beauty is contriving to call up a fmile in its moft graceful form, fhe would laugh faucily in your face, and give you a cannonading from her eyes more immediately fatal to the

heart

heart, then all the foft blandifhments which the faireft face or fineft form can artfully put on."

"And yet," faid Captain Manning, "I admire her companion more. There is a foft and feminine delicacy in her look and manner, that feems to fhrink from obfervation, while the other faucy little gipfy appears confcious of her charms, and endeavours to enthral the hearts of all beholders only for the pleafure of fporting with them."

The tafte of thefe gentlemen was diffimilar, though the warmeft friendfhip fubfifted between them. Their difpofitions indeed were contrafted, but their attachment was fincere and ardent.

There was juft fufficient of the athletic in Captain Melford's perfon to take from it all appearance of effeminacy, and fpeak him fit for the profeffion he had chofen. Did

we

we dare to contradict the assertion of that great author, Goldsmith, who has declared there are no such things as black eyes, but that particular rays of light reflecting on those orbs give them that hue, we should have pronounced his to be of that colour. Giving up our opinion, however, to one far, far indeed, more skilled in the phœnomena of nature than ourselves, we shall say that his eyes were of the darkest hazel. His features could not boast of harmonious symmetry; but there was an irresistible expression in them that evinced a soul fraught with fire and vivacity. His understanding was brilliant. A great degree of volatility led him into all the fashionable dissipations of the age; and a portion of good and bad qualities were so nicely blended in his character, that his enemies could scarcely point out his defects, or his friends censure

them,

them. He was ambitious, and impetuous; but the exercife of thefe paffions was checked by a great fhare of levity mixed with exceffive generofity. To the moft fubtle infinuation he joined a talent for fatire, which he never fcrupled to indulge, except, indeed, on thofe depreffed by poverty, or labouring under any natural imperfection. A large portion of vanity gave an eafy and elegant affurance to his manners, and contributed to maintain the air of confcious fuperiority it infpired. His converfation was univerfally thought agreeable, his company continually courted, and by the fair fex he was efteemed irrefiftible. The foul of this young man was a luxuriant foil, where every goodnefs might have flourifhed, had not diffipation, by an infenfible inroad, fullied its native purity. A prevailing love of gallantry had taught him all thofe feducing wiles which

have

have made fo many innocents for ever
wretched. Virtue however could not wholly
defert a heart where her faireft, her moft fa-
voured child, Philanthropy, unalterably
remained.

Captain Manning, with as bewitching
an infinuation as Melford, had not the inclination to render it fo dangerous. A ftrict
adherence to moral principle influenced all
his actions. Poffeffed of exquifite fenfibility,
exalted honour, and tender benevolence, he
regarded women as unprotected beings,
formed to alleviate fublunary cares, and de-
pending on man for their fupport. From
the nobleft fentiments, therefore, that can
adorn the human mind, and not from coldnefs of heart, he deemed feduction a crime
which no example could authorize, no eloquence palliate, no friendfhip excufe. The
generality of obfervers efteemed him handfome.

ſome. There was a ſoft luſtre in his eyes which, Yorick would have pronounced, denoted a man who made love by ſentiments. He had, in truth, as Fielding has expreſſed it, as much of the " human angelic" about him as it is poſſible to conceive.

Pleaſed with the adventure they had met with, they toaſted in Champaign, ſparkling as their eyes, their fair unknown, whoſe name, ſituation, and genealogy, Melford ſecretly flattered himſelf he ſhould ſpeedily be able to diſcover.

We have now given a ſpecimen of country quarters. Thoſe who diſapprove of it are beſought to ſeize the favourable criſis of a cloſing chapter, and retreat from farther peruſal; as we ſhall give no parole that the ſucceeding ones will be either more entertaining or more ſtupid.

Some

Some, we hope, will good-naturedly make allowances for an undifciplined volunteer; nor at once declare us unfit for the fervice into which we have enlifted; but erecting the ftandard of candour, let its banners benignly float around our head, and gently diffipate thofe fears which as often opprefs the young author as the inexperienced foldier.

CHAP.

CHAP. II.

A FAMILY.

WE shall not, for the sake of mystery, envelop our fair nymphs in obscurity; but at once relate their name, situation, pedigree, and fortune. We shall not indeed ransack our brains, or send others to ransack the Herald's Office for their coat of arms: their family was very plain and very virtuous.

" Virtue ennobles its possessors, and glows with brightest lustre, when grandeur and illustrious birth fade to insignificance." Let the proud lay this awful truth to their hearts.

The

The period will come when their mighty honours fhall be rafed to the duft, and the poor untitled yet virtuous man exalted to dignities glorious as feraphic, lafting as eternity.

Mr. Oufeley, the Vicar of Lanfdowne, was the father of our ladies, and he had one fon older than them. As a man he was beloved by all the country round, and venerated as the minifter of a pure and holy religion, which he inftilled with fervour, zeal, and moderation. His precepts won the heart, while they convinced the underftanding; and affured the thoughtlefs and the gay that, if happinefs was the object of their purfuit, the doctrines he inculcated would lead them directly into the " paths of pleafantnefs, and ways of peace." His difpofition was mild and benevolent, his manners open and accommodating, his friendfhips ardent and sincere.

fincere. The parfonage houfe, in which he
refided, was pleafantly fituated in the middle
of a garden, furrounded by a fmall portion
of glebe, and fitted up with all the con-
veniences that comfort can require. The
profits of the vicarage, though fmall, were his
chief fupport, but the affectionate regard
of his parifhioners relieved him from the
ufual neceffity of watching for their payment:
they felt and revered the merits of their
paftor, they knew the narrownefs of his income, and voluntarily brought in their feveral contributions with hearts of cheerfulnefs
and hands of liberality. Confcious that the
great art of happinefs confifts in confining
the extent of defire to the means of its
gratification, he feldom or never fuffered his
wifhes to efcape beyond the bounds his
humble lot prefcribed; and he was frequently
heard to fay, that the fcience of reftraint,

however

however arduous the tafk may at firft appear, only requires a fteady refolution to render the practice of it eafy and delightful.

There was a faded languor in his countenance that denoted interrupted peace, and refigned content; for, incongruous as it may feem, it is poffible to preferve content after peace is gone; I mean that peace which we eternally lofe on being deprived of dear and valued objects. Our hearts mourn over the lofs of them with bleeding anguifh; but, reflecting on the ufeleffnefs of forrow, the neceffity of refignation, the bleffings ftill within our reach, we fupprefs our murmurings, and are content.

Death had deprived the Vicar of his wife when time was meliorating the romantic ardour of youth into the more exquifite tendernefs of maturity. Attached to her by ties of the tendereft friendfhip, and the

warmeft

warmeſt love, he felt, in loſing her, a link
torn from his chain of happineſs, which nothing earthly could ſupply. For, of all the
ſorrows incident to humanity, none is ſo
bitter as that which is occaſioned by the
fatal ſtroke which ſeparates us for ever from
thoſe to whom love had intimately joined
our hearts. Memory, from time to time, re-
news the anguiſh, opens the wound which
cold content had cloſed, and, by recalling
thoſe joys which are paſt and gone, touches
every ſpring of painful ſenſibility.

Many years had paſſed away ſince her
death. The afflicting event, however, ſtill
remained recent and uneffaced upon his
memory. The laſt look ſhe gave him, the
laſt word ſhe uttered, when ſhe recommended her lambs, her little lambs, to his
care, were ever preſent to his mind, accompanied with the expreſſion of compaſſion,

of

of conjugal affection, of maternal tenderneſs, which overſpread her countenance as her ſpirit fled to heaven, and left her lovely form to moulder to its primeval duſt. From theſe ſorrowful reflections his mind reſigned itſelf to the conſolations of Chriſtianity; and the feelings of conſcious virtue, the bleſſings which ſurrounded his habitation, the faithful fondneſs of his domeſtics, and the dutiful affection of his children, all united in one common ſource of comfort to his heart.

In the domeſtic arrangements of his family, pleaſure was made ſubordinate to regularity, but he encouraged cheerfulneſs, and promoted every innocent amuſement.

His own time was chiefly devoted to ſtudy, except that he, every now and then, ſtole an hour, " when ſilence ſooths the meditative mind," to viſit the grave of his be-

loved wife, and drop a tender tear upon the
fod that covered her remains.

He was not without ambition, but it was
a paſſion founded upon the noble baſis of
paternal affection. He had conceived very
flattering expectations of the future greatneſs
of his fon Francis; and deſigning him for
the profeſſion of phyſic, if his inclination
ſhould concur in the choice, he had placed
him at the Univerſity of Glaſgow for the
completion of his ſtudies. The talents of
Francis promiſed every thing the fondeſt
partiality could wiſh; his underſtanding was
capacious, his imagination fertile, his application unwearied. Certain eccentricities in
his character, however, had gained him, at
College, the appellation of an odd fellow.
His father alfo perceived a high degree of
haughtineſs and impetuofity in his temper,
which it had been the object of parental
anxiety

anxiety to correct; time, he trufted, would
aid his endeavours to meliorate them into
that refined pride and fenfibility, which fo
eminently diftinguifh and adorn the human
character. The breaft of Francis glowed
with all the romantic fpirit of generofity in-
cidental to a young and noble mind, but,
as it was yet untempered by the found
judgment and difcretion of his father, many
fage people obferved that it was a gulph,
in which a fortune, if he had had one to
fpend, would foon be fwallowed up. Poor
Francis, alas! was thoroughly fenfible of the
indigence of his family, and expected no
patrimony but that which might arife in
confequence of the liberal education his
father was giving him. The feelings of
poverty, however, are always delicate and
acute; and the confcioufnefs of his fituation
ferved only to increafe the natural haughti-

nefs of his mind, and to render him impatient
under the fmalleft indignity, or difrefpect.

Rofina, the eldeft daughter, had nearly
attained the age of nineteen. To compare
her with the Venus de Medicis would perhaps appear extravagant and romantic. Her
fhape, however, was finely propoitioned,
and her eyes were certainly irradiated by a
fpark of that fire with which the famed
Prometheus animated his ftatue; for they
poffeffed the power of warming the coldeft
breaft, and touching the moft unimpaffioned
heart. Nature, " with her own fweet and
and cunning hand," had painted her cheeks
with a tint as lively, and as delicate, as that
which blooms upon the opening rofe.   Her
features, indeed, were not perfectly regular,
but they poffeffed a ray of animation which
rendered them attractive. A lovely fmile
played conftantly round her lips; which, be-

fides

files difcovering the fweetnefs of her difpofition, difplayed the fineft fet of teeth, and two of the moft beautiful dimples, nature ever formed, or fancy painted. Her mind, lively and impatient, yielded reluctantly to the flow progrefs of artificial cultivation; and, with a genius capable of attaining perfection in every fine accomplifhment, fhe had only acquired a fuperficial knowledge of them all. The fubjects of her reading had been various and extenfive; but her acquifitions wanted the digeftion of thought; and without meaning to give her the fmalleft offence, her head refembled a repofitory, where different things are promifcuoufly huddled together, with an intention fome time or other to arrange them into order and regularity. This fpecies of procraftination is perhaps of all others the moft fatal. Youth is the feafon when ftudy and application

c 3 fhould

fhould till the mental foil, and ripen the feeds of knowledge into the harveft of im- provement. The gaiety of her difpofition naturally infpired a fondnefs for dancing, and in this elegant art fhe rofe fuperior to moft of her fex. Love of admiration was the predominant paffion of her foul; of courfe the tongue of flattery found eafy accefs to her ear; and fhe liftened to the voice of the charmer with rapturous delight. To enjoy this fweet delufion, the more ufeful occu- pations of learning were neglected; her books were thrown afide, the-work-bag was con- tinually loft, and the harpfichord for ever out of tune. Her converfation, efpecially in company, was lively and unreferved; fhe chatted and laughed, with captivating affa- bility, to all around her; fome of her ob- fervations, indeed, might, from a mouth lefs charming, have appeared infipid; but

the

the poet has well obferved, that "beauty
draws us with a fingle hair." Confcious
charms give a faucinefs to her air. Too great
a love of coquetry made her fometimes
fport with her conquefts. No proud Sultana
could feel a more rapturous triumph at the
increafe of her flaves than Rofina. The
wildnefs and volatility of her character, however, conveyed a fecret charm to all her
actions; and a certain fomething, which,
though I now feel, I cannot defcribe—that
fomething which fo many have conceived
without being able to exprefs, gave a finifh
to her character that was truly irrefiftible;
of what this fecret charm really confifts, I
leave, with other myfteries of importance,
to fome more penetrating genius to unfold.

Lydia, a year younger than her fifter,
was tall, and delicately formed. Her complexion was elegantly pale. A mild ray

beamed

beamed from her fine blue eyes with such
modeſt ſweetneſs, as if " ſecure of all beholders' hearts, neglecting, ſhe could take
them " She was one of thoſe drooping
lilies that ſweetly flouriſh in the ſhade of
ſolitude. Gentleneſs was her boſom friend,
and fair propriety of manners adorned her
every action. Timid and baſhful, ſhe
dazzled not the curſory eye of caſual obſervation, but her ſoul expanded to the
ſympathies of friendſhip. Her ſenſe was
improved by ſtudy; her judgment matured
by obſervation; her principles were ſteady,
juſt, and pious. Suſceptible to every ſoft
impreſſion, her heart melted with ſilent ſorrow to the tale of woe, and ſhe bewailed with
extreme ſenſibility, the fate of thoſe unfortunate beings, who, betrayed by the frailties
of nature, or the treacheries of artful villainy,

he

he obfcured, forlorn, and friendlefs, under the preffure of calamity.

Mr. Oufeley, whofe mind was formed by nature for refinement, had cultivated a very extenfive and profound knowledge of the fine arts. In poetry, the joys and innocence of rural life were once the favourite fubjects of his mufe; but after the death of his wife, he changed the lively pipe of paftoral, for the mournful reed of elegy. Theocritus was difmiffed, and the plaintive ftrains of Tibullus, with Lord Lyttleton's celebrated monody, and Mr. Mafon's two elegies, were the fubjects of his poetic admiration. In painting, his judgment was univerfally confulted, and approved. But mufic was his greateft fame, and higheft pleafure. The voice of Rofina poffeffed great compafs, and exquifite melody. The good old man frequently hung with rapture on the magic foft-

nefs

nefs of her notes. He was anxious to improve fo fine a talent to the higheft pitch of poffible perfection; but he had to lament that her giddy inattention to the rules and practice of the art, was likely to defeat the effect of his inftructions for fo defirable an end. The more fedate and attentive mind of Lydia miffed no opportunity of improving her talents. Her voice was weak, and of no great extent; but fhe played with fuperior fkill and judgment on the harpfichord and guitar; and her knowledge of mufic enabled her, when fhe fung, to give not only proper force to the meaning of her words, but a very delightful harmony to the found of her notes; and fhe frequently revived the drooping fpirits of her father with a fong.

Nature feemed to have formed thefe lovely fifters, as beautiful contrafts to each other.

The

The lively feelings of Rofina were always in the extreme. All her fentiments were influenced by the moft romantic ardour, or coldeft indifference. Characters who did not at once win her favour were filently neglected, but thofe who had the happinefs to pleafe her, became immediately the idols of her heart, and images of the moft exalted perfection. The fympathies and antipathies of Lydia refulted more from the flow and deliberate approbation of her mind, than from the warm and fudden impulfes of her heart. She weighed the merits and demerits of the feveral candidates for her favour in the fcales of reafon and reflection; and indulged or fuppreffed her inclinations, as they appeared to be fanctified by prudence, or condemned by indifcretion. The errors, as fhe conceived them, of her fifter's difpofition, fhe obferved with tender anxiety,

c 6. and

and trembled at the dangers to which she thought they expofed her; but her remonftrances flowed from partiality, and therefore feldom contained fufficient force to produce a ferious effect. The preference of beauty was not given to either of them; for each had nearly an equal number of admirers. Some were charmed by the lively bloom, and auburn ringlets of Rofina, others were caught by the foft languor, and darker treffes of Lydia: and as the cankerous worm, Envy, had never molefted their pure and unfpotted hearts, the moft cordial affection fubfifted between them.

Mifs Margaret Oufeley, a maiden fifter of the Vicar's, only a few years younger than himfelf, formed a part of this domeftic family; and took under her own peculiar care and infpection the management of all the houfehold affairs. She was really as free,

from

from the foibles generally attributed to persons of her age and description as can well be imagined. Her countenance was the index of a contented mind, for either time or philosophy had enabled her to surmount the pangs of disappointment, and except that sometimes she was apt to be a little hasty, and sometimes a little obstinate, none, but those who knew her history, would have suspected that she was—an Old Maid. In her early youth she had read all the novels and romances of the day, and still retained a fond remembrance of the pleasing scenes which they described, but of late years she had endeavoured to alienate her mind from such visionary enjoyments, and repose upon the sublimer strains of poetry, and more comfortable consolations of philosophic truth. The attachment she felt to her brother was ardent and sincere, but she entertained

tertained a higher opinion of herfelf, and her
god-daughter Rofina, than of any two other
mortals exifting.

A judicious obferver of human nature,
Fielding, has remarked, that unconnected
ladies form for themfelves fome pleafing at-
tachments, to which their folitary affections
may repair for folace; and that it is generally
from the tribe of quadrupeds that they felect
their favourites upon fuch occafions. Mifs
Oufeley, with a nobler predilection, adopted
for her favourite a fine young girl, whofe
infancy and education fhe had chiefly fuper-
intended. Rofina had been the little companion of her travels into various parts of
the kingdom, and a degree of cordiality had
been cultivated between them which now
approached almoft to adoration. Mifs
Oufeley's purfe was ever open to gratify the
little vanities of Rofina. Her intereft with
the Vicar was always engaged to procure his
acquiefcence

acquiescence to any scheme of pleasure pro-
posed by Rosina. The praises of Rosina
were her inceffant theme, and her heart vibrated with unusual joy when she heard her
commendations from the mouth of others.
A personal resemblance, however, which
prevailed between them, afforded a remark,
that the pleasures she felt from the praises
of her niece's charms, arose from her con-
sidering them as an oblique approbation of
her own. Whether this remark was founded
in ill-nature or in human nature, is not certainly known. She, however, always openly
declared her resolution of leaving to Rosina
a small fortune, which had been bequeathed
to her by a particular friend, and which her
economy had considerably increased.

Gratitude was among the foremost of
Rosina's virtues; and she repaid her aunt's
partiality by the strictest duty and most affectionate attention. Thoughtless and in-
considerate

confiderate as fhe appeared upon other occafions, fhe never filently fuffered a difrefpect-
ful word to be mentioned in her prefence
againft the character of her aunt. It muft
be acknowledged, that fhe had frequent
opportunities of difplaying her talents of
defence; for every now and then, Mifs
Oufeley gave occafion to fuppofe, that fhe
was one of thofe beings whom nature feems
to have created more for the purpofe of
affording amufement to others, than of receiving pleafure herfelf. But thefe little
oddities in her temper were of fhort duration,
and Rofina almoft doubted their exiftence,
for, in her eyes, to be her friend was always
to be faultlefs.

In the garden of the Vicarage there was
a fhed, " o'ercanopied with lufcious wood-
bine," and furrounded by oaks, whofe broad
and antique branches, profufely encircled
with ivy, fheltered it from the fun, and
spoke

spoke it the seat of ancient friendship. This was a spot extremely beloved by Mrs. Ouseley, and now kept sacred to her memory. The redbreast had built a nest within the safety of its shade; and the initials of Mrs. Ouseley's name, carved by her husband, on an old stump, were yet discernible. To this pleasing retreat the Vicar frequently assembled his family, to enjoy the serene evening of a summer day. Here precepts of morality, and instructions of wisdom would flow from his lips; while the succeeding melody of his daughters' voices sweetly responded to the softness of his soul.

The village of Lansdowne was highly beautiful and picturesque. The houses were neat and uniform; and a river flowing on one side of it, gave it an air of luxuriancy and cleanliness. A bridge, built by Mr. Melville, who enjoyed a considerable pro-

perty

perty in the neighbourhood, increafed the beauty of the landfcape.

The Vicarage houfe was built upon a lawn, furrounded with flat and rifing fpots of ground. Small clumps of various kinds of trees, were placed at pleafing diftances from each other, grouped with evergreens and perennial fhrubs, whofe different tints gave an air of richnefs and cultivation to the fcene. One wing of the houfe was almoft obfcured by a grove; the other prefented a neat appearance to the road, from -which it was only feparated by a quickfet hedge. The gardens were equally formed for pleafure, utility, and retirement. The river meandering at their foot, gave to the adjoining lands fertility and verdure; and thofe ftars of the earth, as Cowley ftyles the painted populace of nature, wantoned

toned in parterres, and crept from beneath hedges of eglantine and myrtle. Two ſtumps of trees formed a grotefque bridge over the river, and led into a field which was divided from the garden by a ſlight paling. In this field was a cottage, where a family lived, whom Mr. Oufeley's humanity had pre-ferved from ſtarving. They now indeed ſubſiſted partly by his bounty, and partly by the induſtry he afforded them the means of exerciſing. But they were contented and happy.

The head of this family was a very old man, whoſe long grey locks commanded involuntary reſpect. He was the chronicle of the village, and could recount anecdotes of all that had paſſed for more than half-a century. Lydia paid him many viſits, and has ſat whole hours with him under a haw-

thorn

thorn bush, upon a bench which he himself had made, listening, with admiration, to his tales.

We have now introduced our readers to the Ouseleys, a family which, we hope, will not be unpleasing to them. The picture we designed to exhibit, rough and imperfect as this sketch of it may be, will present an outline, to the virtuous and tender hearted at least, which the benevolent feelings of their own bosoms will fill up. The tints will be supplied in proportion to the warmth and fancy of the several artists. The subject, however, we trust, will so forcibly affect the heart, that, while the mind owns the blessings bestowed upon the Vicar's humble roof to be just, the tongue will exclaim, in the beautiful and affecting language of the poet,

" Blest

" Bleſt be that ſpot, where cheerful gueſts retire,

" To pauſe from toil, and trim their evening fire;

" B'eſt that abode, where want and pain repair,

" And every ſtranger finds a ready chair,

" Bleſt be thoſe feaſts, with ſimple plenty crown'd,

" Where all the ruddy family around

" Laugh at the jeſts, or pranks, that never fail,

" Or ſigh, with pity, at ſome mournful tale,

" Or preſs the baſhful ſtranger to his food,

" And learn the luxury of doing good.

GOLDSMITH.

CHAP

CHAP. III.

AN INVITATION.

THE morning after the adventure with
the Officers, Rofina was fettling fome flowers
at the window which looked into the road,
when two gentlemen paffed by, from whom
fhe received a very polite falute. " Oh
Lydia!'" fhe exclaimed, in an ecftacy, " as
I live, there are the Officers, you may be
fure they come this way on purpofe to fee
us."

Lydia

Lydia very gravely remonftrated with her fifter on the impropriety of having allowed thofe young men to accompany them home.

" Will you never learn prudence, Rofina?" faid fhe, " I am fure you muft confefs that your fright laft night was all pretence; for I have often feen you meet droves of cows without the leaft fear, and laugh at me if I expreffed any."

" My dear Lydia," replied Rofina, " does not papa always defire us to do as we would be done by? Suppofe now you and I had fet our hearts on knowing two very pretty fellows, fhould we not be extremely obliged to them for affording us the opportunity of gratifying our inclinations?"

Sufan, the fervant-maid, who had juft come from milking, haftily laying down her pail, at this moment, ran into the parlour. " Oh lud! my ladies," cried Sufan, " who would

would have thought it? two fine gentlemen came into the field to me while I was milking. One of them wanted to kifs me; nay, for that matter, he did kifs me. 'And fo, Sir,' fays I, 'though I be a poor girl, I never lets any one be rude.' 'Why, child,' fays he, 'fure we are privileged.'—Indeed, my ladies, he was a mighty fine, handfome man.—— 'Well now, my pretty lafs,' fays one of them, 'do you know who lives in that houfe?' 'Certainly I do,' fays I, 'when it is my own mafter's.' So then he afked the world and all of queftions."

"Did you tell him who we were?"

"Aye, that I did; 'and let me fee,' fays I, 'who beats Mifs Rofina, or Mifs Lydia, in beauty?' but when I mentioned your aunt— 'Oh, fome devilifh old hag!' now them were the very words. Don't tell Mrs. Margaret, ladies;

ladies; she would be very angry. One of
the gentlemen spoke——"

" Well, well, he was very impudent,"
said Rosina, " but did he say any thing
about us?"

Here Miss Margaret's footsteps were
heard, and Susan ran away.

" Dear Ma'am," said Rosina, in a pretty
childish manner, " Lydia has been scolding
me about the Officers."

" Really, Liddy," said Miss Ouseley, " I
profess, I think you are a very strange girl
to be thus dictating to your elder sister, she
has not lived so long under my care without
knowing how to conduct herself. You have
always been under the tuition of your father.
He is a very good man, but he has not the
taste that I have. Only think, he would have
christened that child Rose, how abominable!
but I absolutely insisted on her being called

Rofina. Rofina is a foft and pretty appellation, and looks tolerable enough at the
bottom of a letter. I have read, child, I
have read, books have improved my judgment; I have drank deep, as my dear Pope
fays, of the Pierian fpring; but I never
boaft. I fuffer my talents to lie hid in obfcurity, like the bloffoms of fpring in embryo,
till the difcernment of others, like the expanding gale, draws them forth to full perfection.
It was very natural, my dear, for the Officers
to be ftruck with your fifter, and with you
too, for you are really pretty   There is no
one elfe in the village worth their knowing.
A Vicar's family in every place is refpectable.
I dare fay they had heard of us, of us all,
my dear. You know Mr. Collins gets acquainted with every one in a moment. I
fairly confuted all his arguments the other
evening;

evening; and I dare fay, he has told every body how cruelly I routed him."

Juft as this learned harangue concluded, Mr. Oufeley entered from his morning walk, in which he conftantly paid fome benevolent vifits, and the family fat down to breakfaft.

The morning was paffed in its ufual harmony; but in the afternoon, a long converfation in Mifs Margaret's chamber, between her and Rofina, convinced Lydia that that fome grand fcheme was in agitation; efpecially when Sufan was difpatched with a pattern of blue ribbon to purchafe fome of the fame fort from a haberdafher on the parade. She readily conjectured, that the important object of the confederacy was to ftorm the Officers' hearts; an enterprife in which fhe was confcious her aunt would act as an auxiliary. When they appeared at tea, the ribbon was difcovered to ornament a

D 2   chip

chip hat for Rofina, and to make a large top-knot for a very fine laced hood of Mifs Margaret's, which feldom made its appearance except on important occafions.

To the parade they repaired. The little coquettifh heart of Rofina fluttered at the fight of her beaux, who inftantly came up, and, paying their compliments with the moft flattering politenefs, joined the party with eafy familiarity.

Mifs Margaret foon convinced them that the formidable dragon they had conjured up in the form of an old maid to guard the Hefperian fiuit, did not really exift. She chatted to them with the greateft affability and good-humour, and, on quitting the parade, invited them, with a young Officer of the party, to fpend the following evening at the Vicarage—an invitation which rather furprifed Lydia, but it had been previoufly

refolved

resolved upon between Miss Margaret and Rosina.

Captain Melford, Captain Manning, and their young military friend, attended the ladies home. Miss Margaret asked them in, but did not press the invitation, as she observed her brother walking on the lawn, and knew that he had no very favourable sentiments of military men: a most unhappy prejudice, which she had vainly endeavoured to eradicate; and which obliged her to consider in what manner she should best disclose to him the intimacy she had formed with them, and her intention to encourage their visits at the Vicarage.

The Officers, bidding their fair friends adieu, marched back to quarters. "Well, Manning," cried Melford, "are we not in luck? what a delicious little gipsy! such eyes! such lips! so enchantingly wild! what

think

think you now, Welford, of thefe natural curiofities? would you hang them up with your uncle's petrified mufcles and dried mandrakes?"

" Poft me in Coventry!" replied Welford, " but I think her irrefiftible. She has more fire than I ever faw woman poffefs. The other is indeed what you call ftill life, a fpecies of automaton."

" Upon my honour," faid Manning, " were I to give my opinion, I fhould fay that fhe has more expreffion in her countenance than her fifter. She is not indeed quite fo dazzling; but her looks are more infinuatingly fweet."

" Aye, 'thofe looks demure that deeply pierce the foul," cried Melford. " But come, there is a party in my room for *vingt un*; Welford himfelf fhall officiate as Ganymede; and in Burgundy, my boys, ruddy as the

cheek

cheek of her I love, though not so exquisite as nectar, we will toast the lovely charmers."

"Who are those gentlemen that I saw at the door just now?" said Mr. Ouseley to his sister.

"Gentlemen!" answered she, with a flirt of her head, "why, very pretty gentlemen, my dear, they are some of the Officers who are lately come to Lansdowne."

"Margaret," replied the Vicar, "you know that I do not wish my girls to form any intimacy with the military: the profession is certainly honourable, but the members of it are too often libertines, who care not how much they embitter the peace of a family."

"Really, Sir," said she, "I thought that you had a higher opinion of your daughters' discretion. Besides, Sir, you should consider, yes Sir, you should consider me and

my

my example. You can't think that I am included in the vulgar saying, ' that red coats are as deſtructive to women, as red bait is to gudgeons."

In this ſtrain ſhe continued for a conſiderable length of time, for to do her juſtice, taciturnity could not be reckoned among the number of her faults. Mr. Ouſeley, who loved quietude, and thought it well purchaſed by ſubmiſſion, gave up the contention. She was not, however, a generous enemy; for her brother never yielded any point to her, but ſhe repreſented to him the abſurdity of ever having contended it with her.

This converſation paſſed as they ſauntered on the lawn. They now entered the houſe; and the Vicar, pulling a chair to the fire, lighted his pipe. Miſs Margaret, however, continued to ring ſuch a peal in his ears, that at laſt it diſcompoſed his temper, and,

pulling

pulling the pipe from his mouth, he gave her such an unexpected whiff as effectually filenced her.   She was feized with a violent fit of coughing, and abruptly left the room, muttering the heavieft invectives againft the fmoaky nation of the Dutch, whom fhe ftigmatized as the firft planters of tobacco.

Lydia foon after came into the room with her father's fupper.   It confifted of a roll and a fmall cream-cheefe, of which he was remarkably fond, and fhe generally had one, made by herfelf, ready for him againft night.   While he was eating his humble meal, he defired her to read Gray's Elegy in a Country Church-Yard.   The tears gliftened in his eyes as fhe proceeded; but at this verfe, they fell on his cheek :

"Can ftoried urn, or animated buft,

"Back to its manfion call the fleeting breath?

"Can honour's voice provoke the filent duft,

"Or flattery footh the dull cold ear of death?"

He

He fighed; the foftnefs of her whom he had loft was uppermoft in his foul. Lydia was affected. "I won't read any more to-night, papa," faid fhe, "I muft fing you a little air which Rofina has taught me." She accordingly took up her guitar and fung it. Her father kiffed her, called her his cherub, and, bleffing her, retired to his apartment.

The next morning Mifs Margaret was immerfed in preparations for the reception of the Officers. Had Hogarth been alive, and wanted to delineate the picture of a Lady Mayorefs employed in preparing an entertainment for the cits, he would probably have taken the outline of it from Mifs Oufeley.

While fhe was thus bufied, a lady arrived to pay her a vifit. This lady was a Mrs. Norris, who refided in the village, between whom and Mifs Margaret a very fpirited emulation

emulation fubfifted. There was that con-
geniality between them which is often far
from producing mutual efteem. Pretty much
on an equality in fenfe, merit, and other
perfections, they entertained a wifh and a
hope of rifing above each other. In truth,
a fincere and cordial averfion fubfifted between them; though they frequently vifited,
and fometimes fipped tea, in feeming harmony, from the fame board.

Mrs. Norris had two daughters, whofe
beauty was unqueftionable; and many
thought them equal to the Vicar's. This
comparifon, however, always provoked Mifs
Margaret's indignation, and fhe took every
opportunity of fetting up her nieces in
oppofition to the Mifs Norrifes, extolling
their charms, exaggerating the number of
their admirers, and lamenting the perfecution
the poor girls fuffered from thofe whofe

addreſſes they were, from want of inclination, abſolutely compelled to diſcourage.

To be caught in ſuch a ſcene of confuſion by ſuch a goſſip as Mrs. Norris, was inſupportable. Some one has ſaid that there are white lies, which are not very heinous; and, I ſuppoſe, Miſs Margaret was of this opinion, as ſhe had always declared to Mrs. Norris that ſhe left pickling, preſerving, and ſuch ſort of things, wholly to her brother's houſe-keeper. In fact, ſhe herſelf officiated in that capacity; for her brother's income was not calculated to ſupport the expence or parade of ſuch domeſtic appendages.

Slipping, therefore, ſoftly up ſtairs, ſhe put on a clean hood, handkerchief, and apron, and taking a book in her hand, marched very deliberately into the parlour.

"Excuſe

"Excuſe me, my dear neighbour," ſaid ſhe, "but when I am once deeply engaged upon the ſubject of the ſublime and beautiful, I always leave it with regret."

"Oh, Ma'am," cried Mrs. Norris, "I beg you will make no apology. When I am myſelf engroſſed by ſuch refined ſtudies, I hate to be interrupted. I am ſure, had I known how well you were employed, I ſhould have made it almoſt a ſcruple of conſcience to have intruded on you."

"Dear Mrs. Norris, you are ſo good, I am ſure I am particularly obliged to you for this viſit, when I am indebted two viſits to you, but we have been ſo much engaged of late. Were you at the Granthams? oh no! I recollect you were not, I was vaſtly ſorry that we had not the pleaſure of ſeeing you there; but now I recollect, there is a coolneſs between you and ſome part of that worthy

worthy family. Well, as I say to my brother, it is foolish to quarrel upon trifling occasions. I acknowledge I like to keep fair with every one."

The real intention of Mrs. Norris's visit, was to learn by what means the Miss Ouseleys had acquired such an intimacy with the Officers, and to vent her feelings against them, for having neglected to give the preference to her daughters.

" So, Ma'am," says she, " I hear you have got acquainted with the Officers; upon my word, I believe you'll not find it very eligible; they say they are a dangerous idle set; I know I would not allow my girls to have any thing to say to them."

" I commend your prudence very much," said Miss Margaret, with a titter; " but, thank God, I have no reason to be afraid of my girls. Indeed they were so impor-

tuned

tuned to fuffer an introduction, that it could not be avoided. Poor things! I am fure they feel fufficiently for the pain they involuntarily give to others. I am fure, I think at leaft, that there are people equal to them; but opinions upon this fubject will differ, and there is no accounting for tafte. 'Sir,' fays I to a gentleman the other day, 'there are girls in the village very fuperior to my nieces. I cannot conceive why you, and all the gentlemen, fhould be dancing continually after them.'—'No, Madam, that is impoffible,' cried he, 'mortal eyes never beheld fuch charming creatures, fuch tranfparent complexions, fuch florid blooms! Lydia fo like a turtle dove, and Rofina fo like what you have been, nay, what you ftill are.'—'Indeed, Sir,' faid I, 'I muft acknowledge that I think them very handfome.'—'Every girl in the village is a ruftic to them,' replied he.

he. 'Oh, Sir!' cried I, 'the Miss Norrises, sure——''

" Yes, the Miss Norrises," said their
mother, ready to burst with indignation.

But she was prevented from venting it, by
a violent scream which issued from the
kitchen, and called Miss Margaret hastily
from the parlour. A large bowl of cream
had been left on the hob of the kitchen fire-
place, which the sagacious nostrils of a cat had
unfortunately discovered. Susan perceiving
the danger to which this rich collection was
exposed, had endeavoured to save it, but,
in her fright, overturned a saucepan of
plumbs, which were stewing on the fire.

Fielding has noticed the remark of some
wise men, that misfortune never comes
single, and the truth of the apothegm, in
the present instance, almost soured the sweet-
ness of Miss Margaret's temper, but, recollecting

collecting her vifiter above ftairs, fhe compofed her fpirits, and returned into the
parlour. During her abfence, Mrs. Norris
had happily fmothered her rage, and they
parted with as cordial a hatred, and as much
politenefs, as ever.

Mr. Oufeley was yet unacquainted with
the 'coming of the expected guefts, but as
the hour, of their arrival approached, it became neceffary to confult what meafures were
the moft expedient to be adopted upon fo
critical an emergency. A fynod therefore
was fummoned in Mifs Margaret's room,
and, after much argument and great delibe-
ration, it was agreed to take him by furprife.
The arm-chair, in which Mr. Oufeley
ufually flumbered after dinner, was the in-
ftrument by which this meafure was to be
carried into execution. The cover of it
had been worked by his wife, and it was'
generally

generally the firft objeƈt to which he direƈted his eyes on entering the room. But, when he came in to dinner, he looked, and looked in vain, for his chair.

"Brother," cried Mifs Margaret, with a fmile on her face, "you are looking for what you cannot find."

"So I perceive, fifter; but the age of miracles is paffed, and I cannot fancy that my chair has been removed by the hand of magic."

"No, indeed," faid fhe, "it was by my orders. We expeƈt company this evening."

During dinner-time an explanation enfued. The Vicar warmly remonftrated, and Mifs Margaret as warmly petitioned and protefted, until he gave up the point. He declared, however, that an intimacy with the Officers muft not be encouraged.

Pleafed

Pleafed with the thoughts of his girls being happy, he foon refumed his good-humour; to which the arch faucinefs of Rofina not a little contributed. Kiffing them both, he called them idle flirts, faid he would leave to themfelves, enjoy a *téte-à-téte* with Horace, and call afterwards on Mr. Sedgeley.

" And pray, papa," faid Rofina, " tell him that I am very angry with him; he has not been here thefe three days. If he goes fo often to vifit Mifs Mills, I fhall be tempted to fend her an Italian prefent."

" Aye," cried Mifs Margaret, " and tell him that the falling out of lovers is the renewal of love."

The moment the Vicar had left the houfe the Officers appeared at the gate, Rofina flew to the glafs, Lydia herfelf took a fly peep at it, and Mifs Margaret, fmoothing a

wrinkle

wrinkle in her apron, prepared to receive them in due form.

And now, if any pretty little Mifs, who is perufing thefe pages, fees any pretty little beau whom fhe admires, we beg that fhe, may difcard the book, for the prefent, and give him a very civil reception.-

CHAP.

CHAP IV.

THE ENTERTAINMENT.

THE company were introduced into the beſt room, where every thing had been previouſly prepared, and placed in great order, for their reception. The converſation, as we may naturally ſuppoſe, ſoon became extremely brilliant. Miſs Margaret ſeized every opportunity to diſplay the vaſt extent of her underſtanding. Roſina coquetted with admirable dexterity. Lydia fell into a

kind

kind of fentimental flirtation with Captain Manning.

"I am afraid, gentlemen," faid Mifs Oufeley, "that you find Lanfdowne rather dull and ftupid."

"There are fo many delightful refources in its environs, Madam," faid Melford, "that whoever pronounces it dull, muft be entirely devoid of tafte" While he uttered this obfervation his eyes were fixed on Rofina, and fhe perfectly underftood their meaning.

"Oh, you gentlemen of the Army," anfwered Mifs Margaret, "are fo extravagantly polite! I had an uncle, Sir, and he ufed to fay to me, 'Margaret, my dear, if ever you fhould marry and have a fon, fend him into the Army; it is the only fchool of true and genuine refinement."

"How

" How fenfibly then, Madam, ought we
to regret your difinclination to matrimony!"
cried Melford. " The fon of a lady of fuch
fupreme merit, and high accomplifhments,
muft have conferred diftinguifhed honour on
the profeffion."

" Ah, Sir!" replied Mifs Margaret, in
a kind of figh, " there is, I am perfuaded,
a particular deftiny which directs thefe
affairs."

" There are, I am convinced, Madam,"
exclaimed Manning, while he looked at
Lydia, " real Divinities, who prefide over,
and direct every emotion of the human
foul, whofe decrees in determining our fate,
are, in my opinion, much more powerful
and extenfive than thofe afcribed to the
Deftinies by the heathen mythology."

The idea of the heathen mythology ope-
rated like a charm upon the mind of Mifs
Oufeley.

Oufeley. She had read, with fome attention, the hiftory of the Pantheon; and it appeared to her a fubject of the deepeft erudition. Proud of difplaying her abilities upon all occafions, fhe feized the prefent opportunity with particular pleafure, and immediately entered into a long harangue upon the nature of the feveral deities of the heathen world. From thefe premifes, fhe deduced, by a fpecies of rhetorical ingenuity peculiar to herfelf, the injuftice of thofe punifhments which Fate frequently inflicts by the means of involuntary agents, and inftanced the pangs of immutual or defpifed love, hinting at the fame time, with feeming lamentation, the number of admirers who, very unintentionally on her part, had fuffered from the too powerful influence of her own charms, and concluding with fome fignificant remarks on the difadvantages of too refined a tafte, the

capricious

capricious nature of which had prevented her, notwithftanding the many opportunities fhe had had, from making the matrimonial choice which her mind would have approved.

The coldnefs of a converfation merely fentimental, was not likely, under any circumftances, to pleafe fo young and lively a fociety for any length of time. The condenfing power, therefore, of Mifs Oufeley's fpeech, produced an effect fomething like that of petrifaction, and at once fufpended the faculties of her audience. A momentary filence prevailed. She at length lamented that fhe had not a party for cards, obferving, by way of apology, that they had no intimacy with the folks of the village, and that all the fafhionable people of the neighbourhood were gone to the various watering places for amufement. At this juncture a fpecies of diverfion was whifpered round the company, which met with unanimous approbation. It was propofed to play at fome little game, fuch as hunt the flipper, queftions and commands, blind-man's buff, &c. &c. and at laft the paftime of choofing a particular name, to which a correfponding anfwer was to be immediately given, or a forfeit paid, was adopted.

To affert that many miftakes were intentionally made would perhaps be improper. Certain it is, however, that Mifs Margaret herfelf was fometimes at a lofs for an anfwer, and Welford as often obliged to claim the penalty, Melford, giving him a fly pinch, congratulated him on his good fortune.

Rofina, when it came to her turn to be called, laughed, ftarted, paufed, blufhed, and chattered, till Melford effectually filenced her, by fnatching the delicious forfeiture from her lovely lips.

Manning

Manning in attempting to follow the example of his friend with Lydia, was inftantly repulfed. Glowing with blufhes, and trembling with confufion, fhe ftarted from her chair, and protefted that fhe would not play any longer at fuch an odious game. The foul of Manning was charmed by this refined inftance of female delicacy, and his contrition for having offended fuch feelings, beamed with fine expreffion from his eyes; but the attentions of Lydia were at this moment bent only on the ground, and the grave look by which Mifs Margaret intended to rebuke the fcrupulous conduct of her niece, paffed unobferved. The incident, however, deranged the party, put a complete termination to the game, and made it neceffary to devife a new fcheme of pleafure.

The firft confideration in the mind of Mifs Margaret, was, as we have already obferved, to difplay her own talents, the next was to difplay the charms of her favourite Rofina, and fhe therefore propofed a fong. Rofina, pleafed with the opportunity of fhewing the fyren powers of her voice, was eafily prevailed on to comply with her aunt's requeft. She fung with great correctnefs and fine expreffion, and her merit was applauded to the fkies. She called upon Captain Melford, who fung a camp fong. He called upon Manning, who, after fome perfuafion, prevailed upon Lydia to fing for him She accordingly took up her guitar, and fung the following verfes from Goldfmith's Hermit.—

" And what is frien fhip but a name,
    " A c aim tha lulls to fleep,
" A fhade that follows wealth or fame,
    " And leaves the wretch to weep?

" And love is ftill an emptier found,
    " The modern fin-one's jeft,
" On earth unfeen, or only found
    " To warm the turtle's neft. '

The

The soft cadence of her voice, the melody of its trill, the paufe—the emphatic paufe which she made at the laft line, were inexpreffibly beautiful.

Manning liftened to her with rapture and furprife, new beauties rofe every moment to his view—beauties which he had before but tranfiently admired. The languor of her eyes, which denoted a foul of fo much gentlenefs; their humid beams, which crept with fweet infatuation on his foul, convinced him that lovely and fimple nature only, is truly irrefiftible.

" And do you believe the poet?" faid he to her, as fhe finifhed her fong.

" I really don't know," fhe replied, colouring, and withdrawing her hand, " he was a great judge of human nature."

" The affertion, that love is an empty found," cried Melford, " muft be erroneous;

for

for the warm and tumultuous feelings of my own breaft, at this moment, convince me to the contrary."

" The heart of a foldier," replied Rofina, " is always of a combuftible nature, and though the leaft fpark fets it in a flame, yet it foon becomes extinct."

" Barbarous fuppofition!" exclaimed Melford; " but it is the fate of thofe who do not feel, to be infenfible of the pain which they inflict; nor can they be accufed, for

" Guiltlefs of harm, the bright deftroyer lives,
" At random wounds, nor knows the wounds fhe gives."

This rhapfody was accompanied by a foft and tender look, which Rofina returned with a faucy finile. She fuffered him, however, to draw her hand gently under his arm, as the company walked from the parlour to the garden,

garden, where the finenefs of the evening had been for fome time foliciting their prefence.

It was now the fweet, the dewy hour, when the reign of filence affords a feaft to contemplation, the hour fo beautifully defcribed by Thomfon, when

> " Evening yields
> " The world to night; not in her winter-robe
> " Of mafly Stygian woof, but loofe arrayed
> " In mantle dun. A faint erroneous ray,
> " Glanc'd from th' imperfect furfaces of things,
> " Flings ha'f an image on the ftraining eye,
> " While wavering woods, and villages, and ftreams,
> " And rocks, and mountain-tops, that long retain'd
> " Th' afcending gleam, are all one fwimming fcene,
> " Uncertain if b held."

A lighted candle, which ftood in the window of the cottage, threw a glimmering light acrofs the field, through the branches

of

of the trees in the garden. The curiofity of the Officers was excited to know from whence it proceeded.

"It proceds from the cell of a Dervife," faid Rofina, "whom I keep to give me abfolution for all the fins I commit."

"Shall we go to confeffion together?" faid Melford.

"And would you truft yourfelf there with me?" replied Rofina; "how do you know but I might deceive you, and inftead of leading you to the cell of a confeffor, conduct you to a cave fimilar to that of Trophonious? you would not be well pleafed with the metamorphofis it might occafion."

"The cave of Trophonious!" faid Welford, mufing, "why, I never heard of that gentleman nor his cave before."

"Oh! it lies in the fouth-eaft parts of Europe, on the confines of Afia," replied Rofina.

Rofina. ❡ "The beaux, jeffamies, and wild young men of Bagdad were frequently fent to it to be civilized, and they came out the prettieft fentimental fellows in the world."

"I am fure," faid Lydia, "a fhort confinement there would be of infinite fervice to you, Rofina, for I believe you will never grow tame."

Rofina, during the unthinking hilarity of converfation, either faid or did fomething which Melford conftrued into a challenge. She protefted that he had miftaken her meaning; he explained, fhe ran, and he purfued her into the little fhed.

Manning, by a gentle preffure, endeavoured to pull Lydia in after them, but fhe inftantly flew back, and, in a tone of difpleafure, infifted on his letting her go. True delicacy will overawe the boldeft manners. Manning's, however, was not of that de-

fcription.

fcription. He admired, he adored, he revered the timidity of innocence, and to be
its guardian was his higheft happinefs and
greateft glory.

Rofina fcreamed, and, running haftily
from the fhed, told Melford that his conduct
was intolerably impertinent She pulled
fome flowers, which were a little deranged,
from her bofom, and, throwing them at him,
declared that her fifter would be very angry
with him for fpoiling the rofes of her favourite
mofs-tree.   He protefted—fhe ran away—
he followed—fhe laughed—he rallied—and
her difpleafure vanifhed.

Supper was now announced, good-
humour and complacency prefided at the
board. The laughing hours paffed happily
away, but in the midft of conviviality the
moment of departure arrived. The door

was

was opened by the hand of reluctance, and the gentlemen unwillingly took their leave.

Melford, from the obfervations he had made, concluded that Rofina was a confirmed coquette, and therefore thought her a fair object of gallantry. The rational behaviour of Lydia had made a very different impreffion upon the mind of Manning, he revered the foftnefs of her heart, and admired the good fenfe which flowed from her lips. Welford fwore they were both angels. " There is no refifting," cried he, " the quick fire which fhoots from the eyes of the eldeft; and the foftnefs of the other imperceptibly faps the foundation : but drill me, if the old cat, of an aunt, is not infupportable ! May I be fhot if I don't think a vain old woman, one of your has-beens, is more teazing than a fwarm of mofchettoes !"

CHAP.

———————

CHAP. V.

THE PUBLIC BREAKFAST.

To relate the several gradations through which the Officers advanced from a first acquaintance to intimacy, and from thence to familiarity, with the Ouseleys, would be tedious: suffice it to say, therefore, that they were for ever at the Vicarage. Mr. Ouseley was frequently absent, and his natural love of quietude made him discontinue his fruitless endeavours to discourage their visits.

The

The village already refounded with the fame of the mighty conquefts which the Mifs Oufeleys had achieved. The buzzing tongue of flander at many tables, particularly at that of Mrs. Norris, began to join the word imprudence with the name of Rofina. Even Lydia, whofe pure and fpotlefs character the moft poifoned fhaft of calumny could not taint, was only thought more artful, but not lefs indifcreet than her fifter.

Oh! why does that inordinate love of admiration, fo often, and fo fatally obfcure every brighter faculty in the female foul? How often does it caft the darkeft fhade over the pureft innocence, and, miffing the approbation it fo ardently aims at, meets only with contempt! The calm and difpaffionate eye of candour, indeed, will difcriminate the follies of vanity from the errors of imprudence, and the guilt of vice, but

in

in the broad and undiftinguifhing cenfure of
the world, they are generally confounded
with each other. The charms which afpire
to univerfal praife muft be contented with
occafional difappointments, but the modeft
unaffuming manners of humble beauty, always infpire a fenfibility that creates and
cements efteem, and to fuch characters the
heart of man pays the tribute of admiration
with fpontaneous pleafure.

Rofina's rage for conqueft induced her
fometimes to beftow upon Welford the favour of her fmiles, and his vifits became at
laft fo frequent at the Vicarage, that Melford, who poffeffed the conceited wifh of
monopolizing every attention to himfelf,
determined to do fomething to prevent his
any longer fharing that enviable pleafure.
To accomplifh this purpofe, he perfuaded
Welford to write a letter to Rofina, declar-

ing

ing the violence of his paffion; and he promifed to become the advocate of his 'caufe.

The vain and credulous Welford eafily
yielded to the flattering and artful fug-
geftions of his fuppofed friend, and was
not a little delighted by the idea of being
able to boaft of his fuccefs to his brother
Officers; in whofe opinions, however, he
was confidered very little better than a good-
natured, inoffenfive, and inexperienced boy.

Rofina fecretly defpifed Welford as a
fhallow coxcomb; yet, as he added to the
number of her conquefts, and, of courfe,
flattered her pride, fhe receive the epiftle
with fecret pleafure.

Melford had followed the beaier of the
letter to the Vicarage, and Rofina had
fcarcely finifhed the perufal of it when he
arrived. Her vanity made her folicitous
that he fhould fee it. She accordingly placed

it

it in a book which fhe had been reading,
and laid it befide her on the table. On this
book fhe frequently caft her eyes, fmiled,
looked at Melford, and fmiled again. Significant fmiles from her lips he was fure
comprehended fomething. He feized the
book, fhe prettily ftruggled to get it from
him, and in the conteft, the paper fell upon
the ground. The contents of it were as
follow.——

———

TO MISS OUSELEY.

" Have not my eyes already confeffed
the feelings of my heart, or muft my pen
acknowledge that you have taken the cita-
del? Yes, Madam, may my firft battle be
my laft, if I don't adore you! may grape-
fhot be my end, if I don't think you beautifully angelic! may I be pofted in Coventry

every

every day in the week, if I do not prefer your company to all others! Had Helen poffeffed half your charms, I fhould have laughed at a ten years' fiege. Had Cleopatra half your wit, I fhould have thought a fate more wretched than Antony's enviable. Your fmiles are more pleafing than glory or fame; and your frowns more dreadful than the fentence of a Court-martial, or a charge of heavy horfe in the midft of a defile. Oh, award not my fate with rigour! but pity

" the moft devoted

" of your admirers,

" JAMES WELFORD."

———

" This letter, Rofina, is an inftance of your cruelty," cried Melford, " how can you diftract the peace of a poor boy in this manner?"

" Pray,

" Pray, Sir," faid Rofina, " how can I help it?"

" No, Madam," replied Melford, " you captivate involuntarily, and then fport with the hearts you find you have enflaved. but, fuppofe, as I think I know your real fentiments upon this fubject, you were to pretend that this curious letter fell into your aunt's hands, and that fhe, in the extravagance of her vanity, conceived it to be written to herfelf.   Do you write an anfwer to it in her name;   Welford has, I know, a greater refpect for her than you may poffibly imagine, and I will carry on the deception."

Rofina ftarted at a propofal, the adoption of which might eventually place the character of her aunt in an awkward predicament.   But there was fomething vivacious in the idea, highly pleafing to the natural levity of her difpofition—and it was Melford who

who preffed her to comply.   Sitting down,
therefore, together, they framed the following epiftle.

———

TO JAMES WELFORD, ESQ.

" SIR,

" I was, at firft, furprifed at your letter;
but that furprife foon vanifhed when I recollected that the celebrated Ninon de
L'Enclos conquered at the age of eighty.
It is impoffible, therefore, for me, at fo
much earlier a period, to doubt the power
of my charms; but the glory of the conqueft muft be my only gratification. If the
violence of your paffion fhould oblige you
to fall upon your fword, both our names
will be eternized in the annals of renown.
Love would drop a tear over your fate;
while Fame would wreath a laurel for one
who

who could withstand the addresses of a young, an ardent, and an accomplished lover. Tempt me not, oh thou flatterer! let me remain free, nor load my tender heart with the oppressive burthen of an insupportable passion. You are the Shalum who would delude me, like that constant admirer, with enticing words, to alter my state. If I were to draw a comparison between the antediluvian age and the present, may I not suppose the incomparable Princess 'Hilpa, at the period mentioned by the Spectator, was on an equality with me in years? and she charmed, you know, more than one.

" But though I am delighted with the waving of your feathers, and the perfumed breezes of your toupee, I cannot place them in competition with the riches of wisdom, with which nature, time, and study, have so abundantly stored my mind. Think then

no

no more of me. Speak not, write not, vifit not, left the fire of my eyes, more fatal I find than the flafh of cannon, fhould ftrike thee with confufion. Let glory be thy miftrefs. To war! to war! I cannot wifh for the prolongation of your life, rendered wretched by the pangs of hopelefs love. No, I fhould rather pray that the arrow of fome mighty Indian might end an exiftence on which I have innocently and involuntarily entailed fuch mifery.

" May the little weeping Loves and Graces procure a folitary and facred fpot for thy manes! May fome kind hand convey to me thy fcalp, which I fhall treafure with tender remembrance! May thy fpirit, freed from human incumbrance, become, like Ariel, the guardian of your Belinda!

" MARGARET OUSELEY."

This

This letter Melford himfelf conveyed. The confufion which poor Welford difco-vered when he received it is not to be de-fcribed. He read it over and over again, and almoft doubted the evidence of his own fenfes. "What induced the old hag," cried he, "to think that I was in love with her? May I be fhot if I would not fooner fly from her than from a fhell!"

"My dear fellow," cried Melford, "I am afraid we have committed an egregious miftake. The letter you know was directed to Mifs Oufeley, and the aunt, I fuppofe, has received it inftead of the niece. Old women you know are extremely conceited, and fhe has immediately conceived that you were violently fmitten with her. Take my advice, and keep out of her way. Don't go near the houfe, for, in cafe fhe fhould relent, fhe might infift that you had propofed for

her,

her, and either, compel you to marry her, or to meet some of her relations. The alternative might be disagreeable, and expose you to ridicule."

" I marry her!" exclaimed Welford. " Oh, may I be fired from the mouth of a cannon, or roasted on Mount Vesuvius, before I submit to such a fate!"

" Adhere to my advice, however," cried Melford, " and keep out of her way."

Poor Welford was easily imposed on; and though a moment's reflection on the absurdities of the letter, might have convinced him that it was a fabrication, he became at once a dupe to his vanity.

Melford, delighted with the success of his scheme, communicated it to Manning. The aid and assistance which Rosina had given to it called from him some very severe and pointed animadversions on the impropriety

priety of her acquiefcence, but her conduct was defended by Melford with more
than ufual warmth.

When the Officers of the corps were
affembled, the enfuing day, at dinner, Melford called for a pint bumper of wine, and
drank it off to the health of the incomparable
antediluvian Chinefe Princefs Hilpa. The
Officers ftared at the myftery of the toaft,
but the whole fecret was foon divulged, and
poor Welford was faluted by the title of
the enticing little Shalum till quite provoked, half threatening Melford, and openly
muttering imprecations againft his dear Belinda, he abruptly retired, and left his trea-
cherous coadjutor mafter of the field.

We fhall not call them prudes in virtue
who condemn Rofina for what fhe had done.
Partial as we are to her, we muft acknowledge the great impropriety of her conduct,

in being tempted, by any man, to write a letter, the confequences of which might re-coil feverely on herfelf, and place the character of her aunt, whom fhe was bound by every tie of gratitude to venerate and love, in a ridiculous light. but fhe viewed it only as an innocent and laughable frolic.

The Officers, in return for the civilities they had received from the inhabitants of Lanfdowne and its environs, propofed to give a very elegant public breakfaft, to which our heroines received the firft card of invitation. Rofina, ever emulous of dif-tinction, wifhed, upon this important occa-fion, to appear a ftar of the firft magnitude; and fhe employed the intermediate time in various fchemes to render her charms un-commonly captivating.

In Miſs Margaret's wardrobe were ſome very rich and beautiful ſilk gowns, which, in former days, had contributed to adorn her perſon, and extend her conqueſts. On one of theſe gowns, the colour of which was particularly beautiful, Roſina had frequently caſt a wiſtful eye; and ſhe now felt an ardent deſire to obtain it.

Taking her work one morning into her aunt's chamber, ſhe began the attack.

"Well, my dear aunt, don't you long for the pleaſure of this public breakfaſt? I am ſure it will be delightful. The military always render their amuſements enchanting."

"Very true, my dear," ſaid Miſs Margaret. "I ſuppoſe the Miſs Norriſes are to be there. The Millſes are making moſt beautiful dreſſes of lilac. How abſurd is it for thoſe girls to pretend to elegance, without poſſeſſing the rudiments on which it is founded!

founded! you, I dare fay, in a much plainer gown, will look vaftly better."

" It is very true, aunt, that genuine elegance will ftrike the difcerning few," replied Rofina, " but the vulgar herd, which comprifes the generality of tne people, like children at a puppet-fhow, are only ftruck with the beauty of appearances, and I am fure none of my dreffes will produce that effect." `

" Your fentiments upon this fubject are very juft, child," cried her aunt, " and, now I recollect, I have a gown in my wardrobe, which, altered, will become you exceedingly. Ah, Rofina! but I will not boaft, many are the hearts I have fmitten in that drefs."

The pale pink luftring was then produced. Rofina received it with tranfport. The moft endearing epithets were beftowed

on her charming, good aunt, and her little
giddy head, almoft turned with ecftacy, an-
ticipated a thoufand conquefts, while fhe
was employed in altering it.

The fcene of this rural entertainment was
a gentleman's cottage, charmingly calculated
for a *fête champêtre*, which the Officers,
with great addrefs, had procured the ufe of
for this occafion. The fituation of it was
ftrikingly beautiful. It ftood on a rifing
ground, furrounded in the front by a large
fhrubbery, through which various little labyrinths led to a number of feats, formed, with
artlefs texture, of entwined ofiers. On the
other fide it was bounded by variegated
hedges and extenfive meadows.

The river, rufhing impetuoufly over fome
rocks, formed a fine cafcade. The oppofite banks were covered with a thick
wood, the broad o'erhanging and verdant
branches

branches of which were beautifully reflected in the clear part of the ftream, and gave new tints to the water, that rufhed fome yards, difcoloured from the fall. A temple of the lighteft architecture, to which there was a defcent by a flight of fteps, apparently too irregular to have been the work of art, commanded a clofer view of the cafcade. A grotto, which ftood on the other fide, covered with creeping ivy, and encrufted with coral, only wanted a hermit to make it completely a hermitage.

Rufh chairs with cane backs, deal dreffers, wainfcot tables, delft ware plates, birds nefts hung up in feftoons, window curtains of net-work, and fmall vafes of flowers, were the furniture which adorned the cottage.

The long expected morning at length arrived, and a large *partie* very foon af-

fembled,

fembled, among whom our heroines were particularly diftinguifhed.

Rofina was dreffed in the pink luftring, and looked uncommonly lovely. The glow of confcious beauty gave to her lively features more than their wonted animation. Her dark hair fell profufely, in graceful negligence, upon a neck, that rivalled in whitenefs the pureft fnow. A large green bouquet fhaded her bofom, a light hat was fixed on one fide her head, in a carelefs manner, and decorated with a wreath of wild rofes.

Lydia, though lefs adorned, looked not lefs lovely. A white muflin gown was drawn back by bloffom coloured ribbons; and a cap, ornamented with tiffany of the fame colour, added foftnefs to a face memorable for its delicacy and fweetnefs.

Rofina, all life and animation, received a thoufand direct and indirect compliments
upon.

upon the elegance of her drefs and the beauty
of her appearance, flattery, nonfenfe, and
adulation affailed, or rather delighted her
ears· fhe flirted with all her admirers, promifed to dance with twenty, chatted with
affability to thofe fhe particularly liked, and
looked with confcious triumph on the reft.
Her vanity, however, experienced the fevereft mortification.

Melford was convinced in his own mind
that fhe loved him. Wifhing, therefore,
to enjoy the honour of fo proud a victory,
he had boafted to Manning of his fuccefs,
in terms of the vaineft glory. Manning,
either doubting its truth, or wifhing to leffen
the arrogance of his friend, feemed to dif-
believe the exiftence of the fact. Melford,
piqued by this incredulity, had promifed to
give him, at the prefent meeting, the moft
unequivocal proofs of the empire he had

gained.

gained over Rofina's heart. For this purpofe he had determined to devote all his attentions, during the amufements of the day,
to fome other woman, and exulted in the
idea of convincing Manning of his triumph,
by exhibiting to the whole company, the
uneafinefs he was well affured Rofina muft
unavoidably feel.

Men, let them boaft as they pleafe, are
as vain, capricious, and coquettifh as the
fex they admire; equally fond of conqueft,
of difplaying their power, and of inflicting a
cruel pain on the hearts they have fubdued.
Let women, therefore, imprint this leffon
on their minds, that men, in the tyranny of
their hearts, enjoy a fecret fatisfaction in
humbling the very beauty their praifes have
rendered vain.

Rofina, on her part, unconfcious of any
particular partiality, conceived that fhe had
gained

gained great afcendancy over the heart of Melford, and had filently refolved, by her exertions that day, to complete the conqueft. Joy graced her face with the fmiles of triumph.

When fhe entered the ball-room Melford paid no attention to her, but appeared happily engroffed by the company and converfation of Mifs Norris, a perfon whom he knew Rofina particularly difliked. As fhe paffed the chair in which her rival fat, he took the opportunity of paying fome compliments loud enough for her to hear. But he waited with painful pleafure for the effect which he flattered himfelf his indifference would ultimately produce. His heart glowed with rapture for Rofina, and his eyes wandered after her whenever fhe croffed the room. He fecretly envied thofe who fluttered round her; and felt the keeneft anguifh when he

F 5　　　　　beheld

beheld her fenfible of the affiduties they paid. The gratification of vanity, however, and the hope of triumphing at laft, rivetted him to a perfon he abhorred.

Rofina obferved his indifference, and felt the fevereft mortification from his negleft. Her chagrin for a moment got the better of her fpirits, but the natural levity of her temper, the gaiety of her difpofition, the pleafures of flattery, and the pride of her heart, effected their reftoration, and becoming, by their influence, more wildly animated than ever, fhe gave life to all around her.

The contented mind of Lydia was a ftranger to the pangs of a difappointed coquette. She was not, however, infenfible to the pleafures of deferved applaufe, a moderate defire of which is neceffary and laudable.

The

The epithet, beautiful, gave her cheeks a warm and blu'hing glow. Her eyes derived new luftre from the glance of admiration; and though fhe was not fo fkilled as Rofina, " in patching fcandal, repartee," fhe was by no means deftitute of that brilliancy of expreffion, upon which the pleafures of coverfation fo materially depend.

The love of praife has been wifely implanted in the human foul, it is the crowning wreath which urges induftry to attain perfection, and excites our anxious endeavours to place the gifts of nature, and the embellifhments of art, in the moft pleafing point of view.

Manning advanced towards her, and leaning his arm on the back of her chair, faid he could fcarcely flatter himfelf that fhe was difengaged; but if fhe was, he folicited the honour of her hand in the country-

dance.

dance. She had juft promifed a young Enfign. Manning then hoped he fhould be made happy upon the change of partrers, and fhe granted his requeft. He paid her a compliment upon her kindnefs, which, while it called a rifing blufh into her cheek, obtained from her eyes a look of ineffable fweetnefs.

She admired the merit, which her inexperienced heart affured her Manning poffeffed. His fenfe, his fenfibility, were congenial to her own. He appeared to have gained great knowledge of the world. His vivacity was tempered by politenefs, his graver moments by wifdom and humanity. She always blufhed at his approach. Her eyes, the harbingers of every feeling, fparkled as he fpoke. Flattery from him was conveyed with fo fweet a charm, that

it

it excited emotions in her breaſt alarming to the ſafety of her heart.

Although Roſina had given hopes to ſeveral of her admirers that ſhe would dance with them, yet, being thoroughly ſatisfied that Melford would, at laſt, ſolicit her hand, ſhe had not abſolutely engaged herſelf to any in particular.

When the dance was beginning Melford approached her. " Don't you dance, Miſs Ouſeley ?" ſaid he.—" Certainly, Sir," ſhe replied.—" Oh, I thought you could not be ſo cruel as to render ſo many ſlaves unhappy !"—Then, uttering a careleſs compliment he took Miſs Norris by the hand and led her to the ſet.

The tear of indignation ſtarted in her eyes. She could ſcarcely ſuppreſs the appearance of her mortification; but, calling every ſentiment of pride to her aſſiſtance, and

and determined not to give Melford an opportunity of triumphing over her diftrefs,
fhe immediately g ve her hand to a gentleman who had been long requefting it, was
led with *éclat* to the dance, and fupported
her fpirits and vivacity fo well, that Manning, who was ftanding next couple to
Melford, afked him, in a fly ironical whifper,
how he could diftrefs the poor girl fo much.

Melford, irritated by this farcafm, vowed
that fhe was the moft finifhed coquette
exifting. He refolved, however, to rein-
ftate himfelf in her favour, that he might,
by additional affiduity, obtain a more-certain
conqueft over her heart.

She received his firft advances towards
reconciliation with the indignant frown which
naturally arifes from infulted pride. But his
addreffes were the perfection of artifice.
He was acquainted with the moft intricate
labyrinths

labyrinths of the female heart; and well knew how to apply the balm of adulation to the wound he had made. Softened by the humility of his fubmiffion, pleafed by the apparent candour with which he owned her provocation to be juft, and led by the more powerful inclination of her own breaft, fhe, at length, confented to dance with him.

Lydia appeared to be exceffively fatigued after having finifhed the fecond dance, and Manning earneftly requefted that he might lead her to a kind of arbour in the garden, far from the noife of the ball-room, where fhe might reft herfelf without interruption. The truth is, that her fpirits had been furprifed into a degree of agitation beyond her ftrength, by fome very unexpected profef-fions from Manning during the dance. To

the

the arbour, however, she consented to be
led.

A band of music had been placed in the
temple we have before described, and its
martial melody refounding through the woods
produced a fine effect. The waters falling
from the cascade frequently mixed in con-
cert with the found.

The arbour, not far distant from the
temple, was furrounded by a young shrub-
bery of aromatic plants, whose scents im-
pregnated the air with a delicious perfume.
The conviviality of the ball-room was just
heard in a confused and indistinct found. The
retreat, however, was not unobserved; but
the minds of its present possessors were too
much engaged to be disturbed by " the loud
laugh which spoke the vacant mind."

In this arbour Manning and Lydia appeared like two lovers who had withdrawn
themselves

themfelves from the tumultuous, and un-
fatisfactory joys of public pleafure, to the
more refined and exquifite delight of inter-
changing foul for foul, in tranquil, fympa-
thetic converfation.

For a few moments embarraffment deprived both of them of the power of fpeech;
there was a contagious bafhfulnefs in their
eyes very likely to produce reciprocal confufion, Manning certainly looked as filly as
Lydia.

Manning, however, opened the converfation by fome common topic; Lydia anfwered confufedly; and both were equally
uninterefted about the fubject.

Their own fituation, at length, fuggefted
an idea of the pleafures of rational converfe
and temperate amufement. Upon this fubject Lydia, regaining her compofure, expreffed

preffed herfelf with the perfpicuity, eafe, and elegance, of a cultivated mind.

" Society," faid Captain Manning, " is the cement of human nature, by mutual kindneffes it foftens afperity, and by emulation it promotes virtue. The heart of man, created for delight, would pine in laffitude, or grow four with mifanthropy, if it were deprived of focial intercourfe. Our primeval parent himfelf, amidft the glories of a new world, and the charms of a Paradife, found himfelf not completely bleffed, till Heaven fent its laft beft gift on earth, a companion to raife him to the fummit of felicity. I know not which is the moft blameable, the being who ftoically abjures the enjoyments of life, or he who wantonly abufes them: both characters pervert the bleffings beftowed by Providence for the alleviation of human care."

" Society,

" Society, indeed," faid Lydia, " alle-
viates every care, and gives a finer charm
to every pleafure.   The fympathy of affection is a balm for the fevereft woe, and the
bofom of friendfhip is a refource of comfort
to the moft afflicted heart."

" Balmy, precious, ineftimable refource!"
cried Manning, with rapture. " Oh bleffed!
thrice, thrice bleffed is the man, who, if
oppreffed by adverfity, can, in the fweet,
the facred repofitory of a gentle bofom, find
peace, comfort, ecftacy! who, if elated by
profperity, will, from the fame happy fource,
be taught to temper his tumultuous tranfports,
and remember the facred admonition, " that
he who gives can alfo take away!" Oh Lydia,
Lydia!" he continued, feizing her hand in
tranfport, " why, why do we meet but to
part? why do we know but to love? why
do we love, but to feel torture?"

Lydia.

Lydia arofe fiom her feat—trembled—
fat down again—her face was crimfoned with
blufhes. She endeavoured to withdraw her
hand from Manning's—her head funk back
—her colour fled—it was infupportable.

A declaration of love from the man for
whom alone her heart had ever felt a flame,
was the ftrong idea which his warm expreffions implanted on her' mind : a man, pof-
fefling every grace which could charm the
eye or warm the heart, whofe mild virtues
had ftolen filently and unperceived into her
bofom, and infpired a foft and gentle paffion,
which purity might well indulge without a
blufh. A fudden emotion rufhed through
her trembling frame, and fhe felt her body
finking under the tumult of her mind.

Manning, penetrated by her fenfibility,
caught her with ardour to his bofom, and
kiffed away a tear which, at that inftant, fell

upon

upon her cheek. He fupported her for fome moments, but when fhe recovered her fenfes, and recollected what had paffed, a native fenfe of delicacy overwhelmed her with confufion; and, ftarting from his arms, fhe infifted on his immediately conducting her back to the room.

Manning made her no reply: furprifed at his filence, fhe turned fuddenly round to reprove his neglect. He was fixed in motionlefs dejecion; his fenfes abforbed in agonizing thought: a wild and difordered look fat upon his countenance, a pallid hue overfpread his cheek. Alarmed at his fituation, her difpleafure vanifhed. Love, and every gentle paffion crowded to her heart. She felt their empire; and in the warm tumults of her foul, the expreffions, " Manning! oh Manning!" burft, in the tendereft accents, from her lips. He ftarted at the found. An impetuous

ftream

ſtream of ſorrow guſhed from his eyes. He gently raiſed his head, and ſighed. Looking at Lydia, he preſſed her hand, with ſilent tranſport, to his breaſt, and led her, trembling, from the arbour.

Lydia endeavoured, as they walked along, to calm the perturbations of her mind, but ſhe ſtrove in vain to ſuppreſs the tears which ſtole in ſilence down her cheek.

As they approached the cottage, he parted with her hand, and turning to her, exclaimed in faltering accents—" Oh Lydia! ſhould I never be able to expreſs the feelings of my heart, let your fancy tell you what my tongue refuſes to explain."

Lydia entered the room ſcarcely knowing where ſhe was; and when her ſiſter aſked her where ſhe had been, ſhe ſtarted with confuſion and ſurpriſe.

To

To Rofina's thoughtlefs mind her fifter's embarraffment created no fufpicion, but Melford, who was ftanding by her, eafily divined the caufe.

The good-nature of Melford was fometimes mifled by a pleafure for teazing. "Have you been wandering in Platonic delight through the fhades with Manning?" faid he; "or has he been making love to you? nay, don't blufh: it is an old trick with him, I affure you; he makes love to every handfome woman he fees: he has got the prettieft fentimental knack of courtfhip imaginable, but don't mind one word he fays. he is the moft inconftant creature breathing, be cautious, therefore, that he don't enflave your heart."

"It cannot poffibly be in any danger," anfwered Lydia, with hefitation: "The various

various perfections of fo many beaux fecure
it from becoming the flave of any."

The farcafm which Manning had whifpered in Melford's ear on his expected
triumph over Rofina dwelt upon his memory;
and, in plaguing Lydia upon his account,
he felt fomething like retaliation. Had he
thought, however, that his obfervations
would have fo fenfibly wounded her heart,
he would have died ere he had perfifted in
the cruelty.

Selecting a young lady of confiderable
beauty from the reft of the company:—
"Don't you admire that girl?" continued
he, " Manning thinks her divine; fhe is his
conftant toaft. Is fhe not lovely?"

" Yes," faid Lydia, faltering and turning
pale, " I think fhe is."

" Perhaps you think his tafte peculiar.
You look unwell: come, I have been

waiting

waiting on purpofe to dance with you, a little exercife will be of fervice to you."

Lydia begged of him very earneftly to excufe her; but he perfifted in his requeft, until fhe was obliged peremptorily to refufe him.

" It is great prefumption in me, certainly, to expect the honoui of your hand, after it has once been given to Captain Manning," cried Melford, " but fince you are determined to dance with none but him, I fhall only hint to you that it is contrary to the etiquette of the room."

Lydia, conceiving thefe obfervations to be rather ferious, confented, very much againft her inclination, to go down the fet with him. She rejoiced when it was over; nor was Melford forry, for, during the dance, he obferved Rofina coquetting away with Welford. She was indeed enjoying

the fruits of her literary correspondence
with him, by silently laughing at his em-
barrassment, when she taxed him with being
absent from the Vicarage, and hinted that
she knew and was extremely sorry for the
occasion of it.

The entertainment of the morning, at
length, concluded, and the company returned
to their respective homes.' Rosina was perfectly satisfied with the adulation she had
received; but poor Lydia's mind was occu-
pied by new sensations, which alternately
perplexed, softened, pained, and pleased her.
If the words of Manning had been difficult
to interpret, his looks, his agitation, his
feelings were obvious. To be loved by
such a character as Manning, was, to her
artless heart, the highest transport, and to
her unambitious soul the truest felicity.
The words, " Oh! why do we meet but to

love?

love? why love, but to feel torture?" vibrated eternally on her ear. But the air of myſtery with which they were expreſſed perplexed her mind, and ſhe found the pains which alternate hopes and fears produce continually riſing in her breaſt. Serenity vaniſhed, and in its place ſucceeded hopes, wiſhes, doubts, fears, perplexities, and all

" The charming agonies of love, whoſe miſeries delight."

THOMSON.

G 2　CHAP.

CHAP. VI.

THE DISCOVERY.

THE calm and placid enjoyment of domeftic pleafure was not eafily reconciled with the high delights to which the morning had been fo happily devoted. After tea, therefore, Rofina and Lydia walked together to the parade, for Mifs Margaret was too much fatigued to accompany them. The Officers, pleafed with the fuccefs their entertainment had received, fat down to dinner in the higheft fpirits. The rofy wine went round

round in unceafing challenges. The fair divinities they had worfhipped in the morning were now the objects of their idolatry, and their adoration was fo fervent, that when they vifited the parade they were in a ftate of exceffive inebriation.

Rofina, we are forry to fay it, was highly diverted with the rhapfody of nonfenfe which the wine infpired, but the gentle eyes of Lydia turned from them with difguft, in fearch of an object whom fhe could not find.

The fine eyes of Melford were fwimming, not in the foft languifhment of love, but in crazy mifts that almoft abforbed his faculties. His hair was quite difhevelled, the ribbon hanging almoft off it, the powder was fcattered in profufion on his fhoulders, and he looked like an intoxicated Adonis; but intoxicated with the fumes of a liquor far lefs

delicate

delicate than Olympian dew, or nectar from the hands of Venus or her Loves.

He joined the girls, Gods and Goddesses were nothing to them in wit and beauty; and he vowed, ranted, ftammered, complimented, and laughed, until he excited the attention of the whole parade.

Lydia, finking with confufion, and not knowing the dangers to which the impertinence of wild, intoxicated young men might expofe her, conjured Rofina to return home.

Rofina, diftreffed by the fituation and behaviour of Melford, confented. She accordingly defired him to leave her; but he laughed in her face, and refufed.

Lydia, unable to endure fuch intemperate behaviour, attempted to leave her fifter, and return home by herfelf. Juft as fhe was going away, one of the Officers caught hold of her fair hand; and, declaring fhe

was

was an angel, endeavoured to detain her. Melford interpofed with feeming anger, and refcuing her from his brother Officer, vowed that fhe was his angel, whom no one fhould moleft, and he led her in triumph from the parade.

Rofina, notwithftanding all her levity, was-fhocked at thefe tumultuous proceedings; and juftly dreaded the malevolent obfervations with which they might furnifh the tongue of flander.

Lydia, collecting all her fpirits, commanded Melford to leave their company; but he called her a little prude; ranted a thoufand incoherent expreffions about cruelty; and placing Rofina's hand under his arm attempted, at the fame time, to lay hold of her's; but fhe rejected the proffered affiftance with fpirited indignation and contempt. The raillery he had exercifed in

the

the morning respecting her absence with
Manning, had not contributed to raise him in
her esteem.   If his gratification was to torment her, she thought it the proof of an
unfeeling heart.   If it proceeded from ignorance of her feelings, it was an instance
of a light unthinking mind.

Captain Manning, by retiring early from
the table, had escaped the fate of his brother
Officers.   Military business had detained
him from the parade; but catching a glance
of Rosina and Lydia as they quitted it, the
moment he was at liberty he hastened after
them.

Rosina walked by Melford's side, laughing and talking with her usual gaiety and
good spirits, while he flourished away with
the bombast of an itinerant player.   Lydia
followed them in silent contemplation.   We
shall not pretend to divine the subject of her
thoughts;

thoughts; but we fancy fuggeftion would not be much miftaken, by fuppofing they were employed about a young hero in regimentals, who had " fighed and looked unutterable things."

Manning, gently touching her, enquired, what could poffibly be the fubject which fo happily engaged her attention. She ftarted; but whether it was confcience, or furprife, or pleafure, or all of them conjoined, that vermillioned her cheeks, can only be conjectured, for the great Searcher, of hearts alone can reafon with certainty from caufes to their effects.

" Oh, Heavens!" fays fhe, " is it you? I am rejoiced to fee you; I have been fhocked, diftreffed, provoked——"

Her fpirits had undergone confiderable agitation; and unable to proceed, fhe burft into a flood of tears.

Manning

Manning fupported her, and endeavoured to footh her feelings. But, in exercifing the tenderneſs of his heart, his foul caught the flame of love, and he exclaimed, " Oh Heavens! how amiable is female foftneſs! Nature has made your lovely forms the objects of our fondeſt admiration; but this fweet auxiliary foftens, penetrates, and fubdues the heart. It is fenfibility's foft charm that captivates the foul. But if thefe powers produce fuch forcible effect on common minds, think, oh think, my Lydia! with what a charm they muſt affect a heart throbbing with fenfibility—too fenfible, alas, for its peace, its happineſs, its repofe!"—A bluſh of pleafure and confufion overfpread her cheeks. It was the moſt expreſſive anfwer ſhe could make.

The deepening ſhades of evening clofed apace, but the obfcurity with which they
threatened

threatened to involve the world, was oppofed by the bright appearance of the moon
rifing in fplendid majefty from the diftant
horizon. The air was mild and refrefhing;
the fcents of innumerable wild flowers gave
fragrance to the breezes, through which
alternately floated the low of cattle, and " the
bufy hum of men" from the village. Lydia
wifhed to prolong the walk, fhe was deeply
in converfation with the man fhe loved,
upon a fubject the moft interefting of all
others to the feelings of her heart. Her
whole foul expanded to the fulnefs of its
pleafures. Her mind approved of the confidence fhe repofed in Manning; and fhe
dreaded the idea of their arrival at the
Vicarage, which would deftroy her happinefs
by feparation.

His words, his looks, were teftimonies
of the moft ardent paffion, and, although

an

an explicit declaration had not yet been made, fhe was confident of his virtue, and thoroughly perfuaded that his intentions were honourable. Under thefe affurances, fhe did not hefitate to indulge her increafing paffion, and the idea of love, even in the loweft cottage, with fuch an object as Manning, was magic to her gentle and unafpiring foul.

They, at length, arrived at the Vicarage. Mr. Oufeley was not returned from his evening walk; and Mifs Margaret had juft ftepped out, by her brother's defire, to adminifter comfort to the wife of a neighbouring cottager, who was then dangeroufly ill.

Rofina, after having fat fome little time in the parlour, faid it was extremely warm, and thoughtlefsly ran into the garden to enjoy the evening breeze. Captain Melford followed her, and they feated themfelves in the little recefs that has already been mentioned.

tioned. Her fpirits had been exerted to an uncommon degree during the whole day, and were now beginning to fink into a foft and tender languor.

Alone, and unguarded, with an object too captivating to refift—an object replete with every infinuating, every beguiling grace, fhe could not refrain from lending an attentive ear to his warm proteftations of an ardent, an enthufiaftic paffion, the truth of which he called on Heaven to atteft.

Unthinking girl! in what a dangerous fituation had you placed yourfelf.—Oh ye Fair! let not the fmooth, the varnifhed tongue of adulation, for a moment lull your prudence.

> " Nor in the bower,
> " Where woodbines flaunt, and rofes fhed a couch,
> " While evening draws her crimfon curtains round,
> " Truft your foft minutes with betraying man."
>
> THOMSON.

A youthful

A youthful lover, kneeling at her feet, and calling on her to be the arbitrefs of his fate, might have drawn from her heart the moft dangerous acknowledgments, but an unexpected object appeared, and faved her from the impending peril.

Mr. Oufeley had beén to pay his cottagers an evening vifit. On his return through the garden, the found of human voices from the recefs ftruck his ears.

The time of the evening, and fomething in the mingled accents which he thought he knew, induced him to approach the place from which they feemed to iffue. He liftened, and heard a confiderable part of the converfation. He entered, and, by the light of the moon, difcovered Melford at his daughter's feet, her hands preffed to his lips, and her bofom heaving with the moft tumultuous fighs.

Shocked

Shocked at the fight, he rufhed fuddenly into the recefs, feized her hand, and, without taking any notice of Melford, led her away, half dead with fhame, and trembling with apprehenfion.

'Melford looked very filly, and twirling his hat about for a few moments paffed through the houfe, made a bow to Mifs Margaret, while he made enquiry after his friend Manning, who was gone, and then departed.

CHAP.

_____

CHAP. VII.

THE PARENTAL ADMONITION.

THE Vicar led Rofina with great folemnity to his ftudy; a place ufually kept facred to himfelf, and into which none of the family were permitted to enter except upon extraordinary occafions. Her heart died within her as fhe obferved her father's countenance, and fhe would have given the world, if fhe had poffeffed it, to have efcaped the lecture that fhe faw he was prepared to give her.

He

He sat down upon a couch, and tenderly drawing her to his side—" I hope," he began, " that I have enough good sense as well as charity to make liberal allowance for the inexperience of youth, and the giddiness of unsuspecting innocence, but I should consider myself as unworthy of the name of parent, if I were to conceal the uneasiness your conduct has given me. The disappointment which I feel in observing you lost to that sense of delicacy which I have ever, with so much labour and anxiety, endeavoured to instil into your mind, creates a pang that almost rives my heart. But I mean not, Rosina, to speak to you with anger or asperity. I address myself to your good sense with the feelings of a parent, and with the partiality of a friend. Reflect, but for one moment, on the danger to which your indiscretion has exposed you. Think

Think of the fituation in which I found you. Who is this Captain Melford to whom you allow fuch freedoms? a young man who till very lately was a perfect ftranger to you, and with whofe morals, character, or connections, you are, at this inftant, totally unacquainted; who, from the vile gratification of his idle vanity, may be induced to boaft, among his libertine companions, of the freedoms you allowed him to take; and in the hours of intoxication and arrogance may, perhaps, invent falfehoods, or exaggerate facts, to the injury of your character, and to your eternal difcredit. Think, my Rofina, of the opportunity you have given him to fully the purity of your fpotlefs reputation; and a woman's reputation once loft can never be regained; like a blighted flower, its reftoration is irrecoverable, like ftars that fall, it fets to rife no more. But I will

fuppofe

suppofe for a moment that a fenfe of honour may reftrain him from making your name the laugh of his licentious companions, the very feelings of delicacy which impofe the reftraint, will deftroy his efteem for a woman who can fuffer him to encroach upon the boundaries of propriety and decorum.

" To fuch a character he may indeed look as the acquaintance of an hour; or he may with juftice confider her in a light ftill more contemptible. But he can never think of her as a wife. Oh, never, never! a very different being would he felect for the affuager of his cares, and the protector of his honour.

" Your mother, whom few could equal in beauty, was the admiration of all obfervers for her modefty and good fenfe. But that lovelinefs, which none could behold without emotion, was, to me, her leaft perfection;

fection; it was her heaven-born foul which gave elegance and dignity to every action.

" Oh Rofina! I hope I have not fpoken to you with fternnefs, but what fhould I have thought of myfelf, if feeing the precipice on which you ftand, I had not cautioned you againft the dangers of your fall?

" My children are my jewels, my only treafures. I do not regret the want of thofe things which Heaven has thought proper to withhold from me: I am thankful for the bleffings it has beftowed.

" When it fhall pleafe my Creator to call me from the duties of this life, to be fur-rounded by a good and beautiful offspring, as it has been my conftant prayer, fo it will form my laft happinefs. I have endeavoured to teach them true wifdom, and if I have fucceeded, I fhall leave them in the poffef-fion of treafures that never fail. Their own

virtues

virtues will then protect them, and enfure them the refpect of the worthy and the wife.

" Come, come, my dear, look cheerful. I fhall endeavour to forget what is paft. I fhall lay but one injunction upon you; and that is, I muft abfolutely infift on your dropping all intimacy whatever with Captain Melford. The military profeffion is both ufeful and honourable, but it is, in general, a life of diffipation and extravagance, and the members of it acquire, by continued pleafure, a diffolute and unreftrained ftyle of manners, which renders them unfit companions for the daughters of an humble Vicar. Their intentions are always ambitious; but you, like your father, muft learn to reftrain your wifhes to the limited fphere in which Providence has ordained you fhould act."

With

With this obfervation Mr. Oufeley concluded his affectionate lecture, and Rofina
left the room.

CHAP. VIII.

A RECRIMINATION.

THE difpleafure of a fond parent made,
for a moment, a deep impreffion upon Rofina's mind. Some parts of her father's
admonition had feverely wounded her pride,
and the idea of being obliged to raife the

fiege

fiege fhe had fo fuccefsfully carried on againft Melford's heart, on the eve of an expected capitulation, was infupportable. Sorrow, vexation, and difmay at once racked every nerve, and tore her heart. She retired to her room, and throwing herfelf upon the bed, burft into a flood of confolatory tears.

Lydia, anxious to learn what had paffed that could poffibly produce fuch diftrefs, followed Rofina into the room. Rofina, when the torrent of her affliction had fome-what fubfided, began to tell her ftory of the tranfaction; and it will eafily be conceived, that from the ingenious manner in which it was natural for her to glofs it over, there appeared to be not much to blame in it. Lydia, however, who fufpected that fhe had given a very fpecious plaufibility to the re-lation, fhook her head as her fifter con-cluded, and made no reply.

Rofina

Rosina understood the meaning of her silence, and was offended at it. " Lord, Lydia," she cried, " you are always so very prudent! but grave people are sly enough sometimes. You may censure me if you please; but I am sure I have often seen Captain Manning as familiar with you as ever Captain Melford has been with me. This very evening I saw him press your hand to his bosom all the way we walked home."

Lydia was unable to deny the truth of this assertion; the blushes upon her cheeks gave evidence against her, and condemned her to a flood of tears.

" Nay, nay, my dear Lydia," continued Rosina, distressed by the pain she had given, " how can you mind what I say when I am vexed? I know that I am too giddy. Don't cry.—If you had told me you had seen

4   thousands

thoufands kifs and prefs my hands, you know I fhould not have thought any thing about it. Papa lives fo fecluded from the world, that the leaft trifling thing affects and frightens him, and he would keep us as clofely confined ás a Lady Abbefs keeps her Nuns."

The entrance of Mifs Margaret interrupted their converfation. She had juft procured a new publication, which fhe promifed to read to them. After the Vicar was gone to bed, they went accordingly to her chamber, and fhe read to them for a confiderable time. Rofina in the meantime altered a cap, and meditated a variety of conquefts by the different forms in which fhe placed it. Lydia cut a landfcape from paper, and wifhed in reality for fuch a cottage, with the object of her heart, as fhe had modelled.

CHAP. IX.

A NEW CHARACTER.

ROSINA went down to breakfaft the
enfuing morning with a determination to
appear very filent and very penfive, but the
unexpected fight of Mr. Sedgeley reani-
mated her fpirits, and fet this refolve at
nought.

Sedgeley was a young Curate, the eldeft
fon of a wealthy farmer in the neighbourhood, whofe pride and affection were highly
gratified

gratified by the virtues and accomplifhments of his child.

The character of young Sedgeley was compounded of wifdom and fimplicity. Nature had given him a tolerable fhare of underftanding, which he had confiderably improved by an intenfe application to the ftudy of books, but his total ignorance of the manners of the world, and a flight tincture of pedantry, obfcured his knowledge, and rendered his learning ufelefs. His tafte in poetry was claffical and correct, but it had given a romantic turn to his fentiments, not very correfpondent with the ufual formality of his behaviour.

Refined love, pure honour, unfhaken friendfhip, were exhauftlefs themes to him; and as he was unacquainted with the depravities of mankind, he was ever eager to difplay the virtues of human nature. Guilt-

lefs

less in his principles, fervent in the performance of his duty, and artless in conversation, he acquired, upon continued acquaintance, the universal esteem of the worthy.

He had professed a most ardent *tendre* for Rosina. Her name was carved on trees ten miles round the country; and innumerable were the sonnets which he had written upon her merits.

Old Sedgeley could give his son a very tolerable fortune. Mr. Ouseley, therefore, had no objection to the match, but he never would constrain the inclinations of his children.

Rosina coquetted with him with the most perfect indifference; and her only motive for seeming to afford him encouragement, was the dear delight of retaining him as one among the number of her votaries, and

to

to prevent him from becoming the choice of any other.

His figure was not unpleafing, the bloom of health and exercife enlivened his features. Fine dark brown hair gave a penfive elegance to his countenance, but thefe luxuriant locks which flowed negligently on his fhoulders, have frequently been twifted by the mifchievous fingers of Rofina into a queue, until Lydia apprized him of her fifter's employment. He detefted novels, and having confuted fome of the moft favourite of Mifs Margaret's philofophic truths, he was not very much in her efteem.

Rofina, during the breakfaft, took a fly peep at the glafs, and told him fhe had been dying to fee him.

"So, Madam," faid he, fipping his tea, " you had a fine ball yefterday! I am told

　　　　　　　　　　that

that all was in the true ſtyle of Arcadian elegance."

"Faugh! Arcadia is ever in your mouth, Mr. Sedgeley," cried Miſs Margaret "It is a great pity that you did not live in Arcadia, you would have made an admirable figure in the midſt of a flock of ſheep, with a ſqueaking pipe in your mouth, and crooked ſtaff in your hand."

"There is no neceſſity, Madam," replied Sedgeley, "to recur to ſo diſtant an era or the pleaſures of paſtoral life. A mind in the habit of contemplating pleaſing objects with that pure, ingenuous elegance of ſoul which Thomſon has deſcribed, will, in this age, ſoon cultivate a fondneſs for thoſe divine pictures of the pure ſimplicity of nature, which the poets have ſo finely painted."

"Our

"Our ball," said Rofina, for that was the prevailing fubject of her thoughts, "was delightful."

"It is the remark," anfwered Sedgeley, "of fome celebrated author, that the military give peculiar charms to every place, in the eyes of the ladies."

"Aye, and he fpoke truly," interrupted Mifs Margaret. She then expatiated, with extravagant verbofity, on the excellence of military characters, dignified them with all the honourable epithets which her extenfive vocabulary contained, and pointedly remarked upon the folly of thofe unreafonable prejudices, which people, who had not mixed much in the world, too frequently entertained againft the honourable profeffion.

The tendency of her comments were too obvious and too important to efcape the attention of Mr. Oufeley, and, rather than

fuffer

suffer them to weaken the effect of any part
of his recent admonition to Rosina, he artfully drew his sister into a full investigation
of the subject, and entirely confuted every
argument which she urged in support of her
opinions. This unexpected defeat in the
midst of triumph, provoked her indignation
beyond controul, and she exclaimed in a
rage, " Brother, brother, your sentiments
astonish me. Do you forget that some of
your noblest ancestors were military men?
Do you forget your descent from the illustrious Douglas? do you forget that your
second-cousin, Jamie Wallace, was killed at
Bunker's Hill? recollect your namesake,
who was blown up in a fortress. Are the
achievements of ancient heroes to be forgot?
the unshaken fortitude of Hannibal! the
matchless clemency of Cesar! the glorious
death of Wolfe! are these exploits nothing

in

in your imagination? do they not warm
your mind? fhould they not fire your fpirit?
That the military, the bulwark of the
nation, the guardians of our property, the
protectors of our virtue, fhould be thus
abufed—provoking!——Was I a man, I
would carry a mufket; and, if I had a
daughter, I would fooner give her to a re-
cruiting ferjeant, than to any fneaking private gentleman, or to any infignificant Curate, with a parcel of homilies in his pocket,
and a rhapfody of poetical nonfenfe in his
brains."

This laft ftroke was levelled, with fome
fuccefs, at young Sedgeley, who blufhed
violently, twirled his cup upon the faucer,
and endeavoured to avoid looking extremely
filly. Rofina enjoyed his confufion for fome
minutes, and then, in order to afford her
aunt a new fubject of declamation againft

him,

him, and to give effect to a joke which she had been contriving, she very seriously asked him if he was yet reconciled to the reading of novels? to which, with a significant shake of his head, he answered in the negative.

"Oh! I suppose you think," exclaimed Miss Margaret, " that you are too wise, but let me tell you, the most sensible people don't disdain to peruse them, and let me also assure you, that those who are ignorant of fine prose, can never be good judges of elegant poetry. If indeed your studies had been devoted, as mine have been, to Milton, Pope, Young, Thomson, Goldsmith, Akenside"——

" The works of those celebrated writers, Madam," said Sedgeley, modestly, " chiefly furnish my library, but the entertainment which they afford, is, in opinion, very different

ferent from that which is derived from the reading of novels."

"Pray, Sir," interpofed Rofina, "what are your objections to novels?"

"The books, Madam, which are in general comprehended under the defcription of novels," anfwered Sedgeley, "are feldom written with any judgment, they fire the fancy without improving the heart, they amufe the mind, but give no information to the underftanding; they promote vice by mifreprefenting virtue."

While Sedgeley was declaiming againft the pernicious effects of novels, Mifs Oufeley obferved a book fticking half-way out of his pocket, and interrupting him, faid, "I fuppofe, Sir, this is one of your admired authors."

"This, Madam!" replied Sedgeley, ftammering, and colouring violently, "no

H 6   Ma'am,

Ma'am, I can't fay that it is an author that I—I—"

His embarraffment excited her curiofity, and fhe determined to fee what book it was. Extending her hand, therefore, fhe drew it from his pocket, and opening the title page, read aloud, " The Fatal Miftake, or the Errors of the Heart." " So, Sir," faid fhe, with an air of triumph, " you hate, you deteft, you never read novels, they fire the fancy, and corrupt the heart."

No words can defcribe the confufion that appeared in the countenance of the afto-nifhed Curate. " The Fatal Miftake!" he exclaimed, in a tone of amazement. " As I live, that was not the book which I had in my pocket when I came from home."

As Sedgeley pronounced this affeveration, the Vicar raifed his eyes towards him with a look of arch incredulity, but, happening

to

to glance them on Rosina, as they passed along, he perceived a sly smile playing round her features, which convinced him that it was in her power to solve the mystery. Rosina, bursting into an immoderate fit of laughter, produced a book which she had dexterously taken from Sedgeley's pocket, during his argument with her aunt, and for which she had substituted one of her own. Miss Margaret, in the heat of curiosity, caught it hastily from Rosin's hand, and opened it with perfect confidence of a new triumph over Sedgeley.   But how great was her disappointment and mortification when, instead of a novel, she discovered it to be an essay on—Old Maids!

"Really, Mr. Sedgeley," said Miss Margaret, "I did not imagine that you had so much hypocrisy. You affect to despise a harmless novel, and yet you can walk

about

about with a book like this in your pocket;
a book written for the purpofe of expofing
to ridicule a whole clafs of individuals. I
have no patience with you'"

"Nay, fifter," obferved Mr. Oufeley,
drily, "don't unintentionally condemn your
favourite author Smollet. Recollect what
pretty fpecimens he has given us of Old
Maids, in the characters of Mrs Grizzle and
Mifs Tabitha Bramble."

This unexpected difappointment very
much nettle'd the fweetnefs of Mifs Margaret's temper, but recollecting that the more
fhe ftormed againft a fatire upon old maids,
the more fhe included herfelf within the
ftigma of the character, fhe fuffered her
anger to evaporate in a fume of fubacid raillery againft the Vicar and the Curate. The
Curate, however, purchafed an entire forgivenefs by prefenting to the whole family
a fet

a fet of tickets for a play, which a ftrolling party was that night to perform near the village, in a barn belonging to his father. The prefent indeed was probably made at no great expence to him, as his father was the Juftice of the Peace who had granted them permiffion to act. Mr. Oufeley, ever pleafed with an opportunity of rendering thofe about him happy, accepted the tickets, and Mr. Sedgeley was invited to dinner, that he might introduce the family with all the pomp which was fuppofed to belong to the eldeft fon of the licenfing Magiftrate.

Rofina's fpirits were immediately elevated by the profpect of an amufement which afforded her the chance of feeing Melford; but her pleafure was in fome meafure abated by the recollection that the company of her father would preclude the poffibility of any converfation paffing between them.

CHAP.

CHAP X.

THE TETE-A-TETE.

CAPTAIN MELFORD had been extremely difconcerted by the unexpected appearance of Mr. Oufeley during his interview with Rofina in the arbour of the garden. The enfuing morning, while he was at breakfaft, his friend Manning entered his apartment.

"How, in the name of wonder, Melford," cried he, "could you torment the girls in the

the manner you did laſt night? you muſt have known that you were in a very improper ſtate to be their companion."

" My dear fellow," anſwered Melford, "you were certainly deſigned as the Cenſor-General of the age. Do you ſuppoſe that they had any objection to me for being a little whimſical? on the contrary, that little wild Roſina ſaid I ſhould be always ſo, for that I was never half ſo agreeable."

" As you have choſen to mention the name of Roſina," ſaid Manning, " let me ſeriouſly aſk you, Melford, what are your intentions relative to that girl? I now perceive, through all her giddineſs, that ſhe entertains a particular partiality for you. Her ſprightly eyes, at the ſight of you, glow with increaſing luſtre. Her cheeks crimſon with a brighter bluſh when you approach; and when you ſpeak, her ſnowy boſom,

bofom, heaving with unufual throbs, indi-
cates the tumults of her heart. You muft
have flattered her hopes with the idea of
a ferious attachment. I know you are no
trifler, you would not feek a conqueft for the
mere gratification of obtaining it, and
therefore you muft, one way or the other,
have a defign; but of what nature that
defign is you can beft determine."

"Pfhaw, nonfenfe," cried Melford, "you
are always fo intolerably grave. I don't
know what you mean."

"Oh! you cannot miftake my meaning,"
replied Manning, "I fpeak to you with
the opennefs, the fincerity, the affection of
a friend, and I conjure you, if your defigns
upon Rofina be not honourable, to decline
all future attentions towards her. The paffion ſhe has now imbibed may, perhaps, be
conquered, but if you increafe it, you may
render

render her, in any event but matrimony, completely wretched."

" Wretched!" exclaimed Melford, with a fmile, " no, no, take my word for it, there is no danger of her being wretched; fhe has not fufficient fenfibility."

" Pardon me," cried Manning, " if I affert that I think fhe has. Were we to analyfe the feelings of her mind, warped as it now appears to be by levity and wild-nefs, there would be found a degree of fenfi-bility, which difappointed love, or the fcorn of the world, would torture almoft to madnefs."

" The generous friendfhip," exclaimed Melford, " which has, from the firft mo-ment of our acquaintance, inviolably fub-fifted between us, has been, I candidly ac-knowledge, the greateft felicity of my life; and I flatter myfelf that it has been mutually

ardent

ardent and fincere. Shall I then, Manning, open to you upon this fubject the inmoft recefses of my foul, fubmit my whole heart to your infpection, and let you read my moft fecret thoughts?—no, I feel I cannot, I acknowledge it is a fcrutiny which I could not fupport. I fhall not, however, entirely conceal my feelings from my friend. Rofina has, I confefs, more of that kind of beauty and fpirit which peculiarly pleafes my tafte, than any woman I ever knew, and fhe has, confequently, received a greater fhare of my attention. That fhe is a coquette you know, and as fhe has been brought up far from the metropolis, it is fair to conclude that this difpofition is rather the indelible ftamp of nature than the temporary effect of imitation. My temper, you know, is haughty, my views ambitious, my expec-tations fanguine, and I own that I look to a

rank

rank in life much more exalted than Rosina's to form an attachment in. Should her love, however, if you will have it that she loves me, tempt me to prefer her charms to the charms of ambition, what prospect of happiness could I reasonably expect from such a character? in forming an alliance with her, all my pleasing prospects of future greatness would in a moment vanish, and I must learn to bear the loss of fashionable acquaintances, and to endure with patience the reproachful sneers of the world. In return for those sacrifices, I should expect, on her part, the most soothing gentleness, the most unremitting attention, the purest and the warmest affection she could bestow, for these alone could satisfy the feelings of disappointed pride, or blunt the sting of pointed ridicule. But instead of these pleasures, intoxicated by her natural desire for admiration, as she

grew

grew more intimate with the world, she would grow more rapacious for its praise. My domeſtic peace would be broken by the caprices of a flirt, by the petulance of diſappointed vanity, or by the flighty conduct of flattered beauty. My private hours would be diſturbed by a crowd of fools and coxcombs, to whom she would diſpenſe the attentions which I should think belonged excluſively to me. Believing her as I do to be a finiſhed coquette, I should be eternally ſuſpicious, and the canker of diſtruſt would be continually preying upon the ſympathies of love. I should think that she was perpetually dancing on the verge of a precipice; and that one thoughtleſs moment might plunge her into an abyſs of infamy, and draw me after as a partner in her diſgrace. Diſappointed of the tenderneſs and attention which I should expect, loſt to my preſent

4　　　　　　　　hopes

nopes and future expectations, I should be tempted to rail against the hour in which I united my fate with her's. She possesses, I acknowledge, beauty and sense enough to conquer thousands, but she wants steadiness and propriety to retain any of her admirers in honourable thraldom. Had she, with her bewitching flow of spirits, a portion of her sister's gentleness, I will not say what madness I might not have been induced, by her beauty and partiality, to commit. But wild as I am, my dear Manning, I can never think of such a being for the preserver of my honour; and while I consider her character in this light, it follows that Rosina Ouseley can never, oh never! be the wife of Melford."

" You seem to think that a connection with the Vicar's family would debase your rank. But by all that is just," cried Manning,

ning, " Lydia Oufeley is a young woman who, mild, virtuous, and attractive, would, in my eftimation, reflect dignity on any ftation. Rank might place her merit in a more confpicuous light; but rank could never increafe her worth, or render her more pure and charming."

" Hold, hold thefe extraordinary commendations," cried Melford, " or I fhall abfolutely form fome ftrange opinion of your defigns. Surely, Manning, you forget that you are already under a folemn engagement of matrimony! but, perhaps, you imagine, what is certainly very true, that fuch a girl as Lydia would contribute to raife your fpirits after a dull matrimonial *téte-à-téte*.—Open your fchemes to me, Manning, and command my fervices, a file of mufketeers or a——"

" If

"If I could entertain a thought," inter-rupted Manning with warmth, "injurious to such spotless purity, I should consider myself the most profligate, the most abandoned of my sex, unfit to exist in human society, and formed alone for unfrequented deserts, and the company of brutes. You say Rosina Ouseley can never be your wife; I hope then you mean to decline all future correspondence with her. It would be cruel, nay barbarous, Melford, to trifle with the peace, and, perhaps, the reputation of a girl who loves you. Consider how it would wring the heart of her fond old parent with anguish, and destroy, perhaps for ever, the serenity of her lovely sister's mind, for on the happiness of Rosina, I know, the felicity of Lydia materially depends—Of dishonourable views I cannot, no," cried he, fixing his eyes ftedfaftly on Melford, " I will not fufpect you."

" Manning," replied Melford, in rather a peremptory tone, " I candidly told you that I could not bear too fevere a fcrutiny. Act as you pleafe with regard to Lydia, but leave Rofina to me."

" Act as I pleafe with regard to Lydia!" repeated Manning, evidently hurt at what Melford had faid, " I fhall act with honour." But he felt that his feelings were carrying him beyond the bounds of prudence, he endeavoured, therefore, to fupprefs them, and, after fome hefitation, informed Melford that he intended to fet out for London early the next morning.

" For London early in the morning!" exclaimed Melford, " when the regiment is to quit thefe quarters fo foon?"

" I am

"I am summoned there upon indispensable business, which requires my immediate presence," answered Manning with a sigh.

"Ah Manning, Manning!" replied Melford, "neither of us, I fancy, are quite so wise as we imagined."—He then rang the bell for the servant to dress his hair, and the *téte-à-téte* ended.

CHAP.

CHAP. XI.

THE PLAY.

SEDGELEY came to the Vicarage to dinner at the hour appointed, and brought with him a beautiful *bouquet*, compofed of every flower the feafon produced, which he divided between the ladies, partially referving the fweeteft· flowers for Rofina, as a filent teftimony of his affection.

Rofina never looked more beautiful, than fhe did at prefent.   Her drefs was in a ftyle of the moft becoming fimplicity.- A white dimity robe, ornamented with dark green
ribbons,

ribbons, added elegance to her shape, a thin muslin cap adorned her head with rural neatness, her hair, curled in the negligence of nature, hung round her forehead, and in her bosom she wore Sedgeley's *bouquet* of blossomed myrtle and rose buds—balmy, sweet and beauteous as her lips. The recent vexation she had felt gave a more delicate tincture to her complexion, and new irresistibility sparkled from her eyes. The appearance of Lydia was equally lovely, though less brilliant.

The tea was ordered at an earlier hour than usual, and, after it was over, the party repaired to the theatric barn, where a crowded audience were already assembled. Among the company were the Officers of the regiment, and amongst the Officers were those who had distinguished them-

selves

felves by their attentions to the Vicar's daughters.

The eyes of Rofina foon caught thofe of Melford. Refolved, if poffible, to torment him, fhe opened a fmart flirtation with her companion Sedgeley, every now and then glancing her eyes at Melford to obferve its effect. Melford appeared thoughtful, penfive, and uneafy, the whole evening. The morning converfation with Manning had difturbed his mind, and his looks always correfponded with the feelings of his heart. In real love there is a fympathy which filently participates in all the concerns of the object beloved, and the difquietude which fat pictured in Melford's countenance foon communicated itfelf to the bofom of Rofina. She attributed his uneafinefs to the circumftances which had debarred him from the pleafures of her converfation, and when fhe

ftood

ſtood up ſhe turned toward him, and gave him a look ſo inexpreſſibly ſweet, as forth at night at leaſt, deprived him of his reſt.

'The play was Venice Preſerved, but no other plot was diſcovered than that which the performers carried on againſt the ſenſe, ſpirit, and meaning of the poet. The tender muſe of Otway called in vain upon Melpomene to defend her favourite offspring from the rude attack. But Thalia invaded her domain, and, heading the conſpirators, produced a roar of laughter throughout the evening.

The entertainments of the evening being over, Sedgeley eſcorted the ladies back to the Vicarage. The two ſiſters were in very bad ſpirits, but Miſs Margaret talked away upon the declenſion of dramatic merit, and paid a tributary ſigh to the revered memory of Cibber, Pritchard, Garrick, and Powell.

CHAP.

CHAP. XII.

THE DANGERS OF LOVE.

THE next morning, while the ladies were at breakfaſt, the Vicar entered the room, and informed his daughters, that the injunction he had laid upon them, not to viſit the parade while the Officers were in the town, would ſoon be at an end, for he had juſt received intelligence that the regiment had orders to march in a few days.

The

The feelings of Rosina were terribly shocked at this unexpected information. Carressed, flattered, and, as she conceived, adored by Melford, she had built a mansion of eternal happiness on the ground of hope which now seemed to vanish from her view like the transient pleasures of a dream. The minutes flew with unusual rapidity; and increasing disquietude tormented her heart as the moment of Melford's departure approached. To part without even an adieu; without affording him an opportunity to say—but, in short, she knew not what she would have him say to calm her agitations. She thought, however, that the interdiction of her father was unnecessary and severe.

Ah, Rosina! how little qualified were you to judge, like that parent, with discernment of mankind. Deceived by self love, the most dexterous and delusive passion of

the

the human mind, you had indulged a thoufand flattering hopes, which the romantic
warmth of youth too fondly perfuaded you
were ripening to perfection.

There was a poor woman that fold ribbons
and other gewgaws about the village, who
came frequently to the Vicarage, where the
girls always received her kindly, and liftened
with pleafure to the arch fimplicity with
which fhe told unnumbered tales. This
creature repaired to the houfe one afternoon,
and, pretending to have a great deal to relate, took the opportunity, while Lydia
was examining fome ribbons, to flip a note
into Rofina's hand; making at the fame
time a fign of fecrecy.

Rofina trembled as fhe received it; and
guelfing from whom it came, was fo con-
fufed, that her agitation nearly difcovered
the fecret which the fign had inftructed her

to

to conceal. She retired immediately to her chamber; and breaking the wax found it was, as her fancy had already fuggefted to her, a letter from Captain Melford.

It contained a very few lines, entreating her to meet him that evening, if but for *two moments*, at the fkirt of the grove, as the regiment was to march from Lanfdowne early the next morning, and he could not fupport the idea of parting without bidding her adieu, and difclofing to her the feelings of his heart.

The immediate impulfes of love and tendernefs left no opportunity for reflection to interpofe. She called to Sufan to come up ftairs, and charging her to make fome excufe for her abfence, in cafe it fhould be difcovered, flipped, unobferved, from the houfe, and hurried directly to the place of affignation.

Melford,

Melford, who well knew that she would
surmount every difficulty, if poffible, to meet
him, was already there, and received her
with all the open tranfport of undiffembled
passion. A perfect mafter in the art of love,
endowed by nature with every beguiling grace,
he taught his features their moft enfnaring
powers. His voice affumed a foft and plaintive tone, finely adapted to the tender feelings he wifhed to infpire, and he foon difcovered the effect which it produced in the
bofom of Rofina.

Some heavy fhowers of rain had lately
fallen, and the grafs was extremely wet;
he therefore prevailed on her to retire to
a little feat, which was fheltered from the
damp, by a clofely entwined covering of
hawthorn. Here he feated himfelf by her
fide, and lamenting the cruelty of their approaching feparation, painted to her the
sufferings

sufferings of his heart in such warm and glowing language, that he nearly drew from the too credulous, and almost fainting Rosina, a declaration of her passion. Observing the ascendancy he had gained, he threw himself at her feet, and looked at her, for a few minutes, with all the speechless eloquence of love. A sudden agony burst from him. "Oh, Rosina!" he exclaimed, "can I bear to leave you? cruel Rosina! how can you behold the man who adores you lying miserable at your feet, without wishing to relieve him?"

"What do you mean?" cried Rosina, astonished.

Again he gazed on her with dangerous softness: a sort of frantic fondness followed; another agony burst from him. He seized her hand with transport, and talked with rapture of unhallowed joys.

Oh,

Oh, Melford! how at that moment didſt thou degrade thy noble character! how darken all the native brightneſs of thy foul! profaning the ſacred name of love, aſſailing the ears of virtue, and ſeeking to plunge the unſuſpecting child of innocence into irretrievable guilt!

He urged his ignominious paſſion with all the confidence of an unfeeling libertine, and with the dexterous, intricate, and diſguiſed ſophiſtry of frontleſs vice. Deep, ſubtle, argumentative, and impaſſioned, he concealed the baſeneſs of his deſign under a veil ſo ſpecious and ſeductive, that a mind leſs ſtrictly virtuous than Roſina's might have fallen a victim to his arts. But although her giddineſs and vanity had driven her to the extremeſt verge of indiſcretion, her mind had never harboured an idea repugnant to the faireſt purity.

She

She doubted at firſt the evidence of her ſenſes; but when he again preſſed his licen- tious eloquence on her ear, ſhe ſtarted up, and, wringing her hands in unutterable agony, attempted to paſs him. " Let me go, let me go," ſhe cried, with a diſordered air: " you have uſed me baſely. Oh! you have trampled on the bounds, the ſacred bounds of honour, generoſity, hoſpitality, and virtue! you have ſought to bring a harmleſs, fond old man with ſorrow to his grave. Could I have thought it poſſible? oh no! of Virtue herſelf I entertained not a higher opinion than of Melford. Oh Melford!" cried ſhe, with a burſt of ſorrow, " how have you deceived me? you have violated the confidence I repoſed in you. You have—"

Melford laid hold of her gown, and en- deavoured to ſpeak.

" Detain.

"Detain me no longer, Sir," she exclaimed with indignation. "Dare no longer to inſult me. The unnerved hand of an aged parent ſhall become powerful to chaſtiſe your inſolence, and I have a brother whoſe youthful arm ſhall make you deeply rue the injury you have meditated on his ſiſter's innocence. Detain me no longer," ſhe cried aloud, with increaſing fury, "my brain already maddens. Let me go, if you do not wiſh to ſee me the ſenſeleſs victim of your barbarity."

There was a wild phrenzy in her air as ſhe pronounced theſe words, which ſuſpended all the faculties of his ſoul. His hands abandoned their hold. She fled from him with precipitation, and vaniſhed in a moment from his ſight. He ſtood for ſome time fixed in ſenſeleſs aſtoniſhment, but recollection at laſt returned. Her image

preſented

prefented itfelf to his mind. The ftart of horror which fhe gave when he firft dif-clofed his bafe intent, the emotions of re-gret, difappointment, abhorrence, and in-dignation, which fucceffively arofe in her heart, demonftrated the integrity of her principles, and bitterly reproached him for the infult he had offered to the fhrine of purity; for the wounds he had given to the heart that loved him.

Never did fhe appear to his view more conqueringly lovely than at the moment when her virtue rofe triumphant over his endeavours to feduce it. Sentiments which he had never felt before, took ftrong poffeffion of his mind. Confcience regained her em-pire in his breaft; the bafenefs and depravity of his conduct tortured his feelings, fmote his heart with the keeneft pangs of guilt, and, in fome meafure, avenged the caufe of injured virtue. He ftood appalled and

self-felf-convicted of premeditated villainy, penitence could fuggeft no mode of expiation equal to the enormity of his crime. He would have laid his ambition willingly at her feet; but, amidft the turbulence of his mind, the ftern paffion of pride interpofed, and relieved his diftrefs. While he alternately fuggefted and difapproved a thoufand fchemes by which he might hope to obtain forgivenefs, he recollected the denunciation fhe had made againft him of her brother's vengeance. His haughty foul caught fire at the idea of compulfive retribution, and all his notions of voluntary atonement expired in its flames. The acceffion of oppofite paffions, however, contributed to increafe the torture of his mind, and he returned to his folitary quarters in excruciating anguifh. Manning was gone to London; and he had no friend near him into whofe

whofe confolatory bofom he could unload the accumulating forrows of his heart; the moft refined and implacable vengeance could not, perhaps, have devifed a fpecies of punifhment more grievous and fevere.

Lydia had obferved her fifter's abfence, and entertained fome unfettled notion of the caufe of it. She was apprehenfive left her father's early return from his evening walk fhould difcover it. Rofina, however, fortunately arrived at the Vicarage before her father returned. She entered the door pale, trembling, and difordered; and, tottering up ftairs to her chamber, funk faint and breathlefs into a chair.

Lydia, who had been watchful for her return, immediately followed her. "What is the matter, Rofina?" faid fhe, in a tone of terror. "Gracious Heaven! what can have happened?"

"Afk

" Afk me not! oh, fpeak not to me, Lydia!" cried the agitated Rofina. " Leave me, leave me, oh, leave me to myfelf!"

" I conjure you," replied Lydia, trembling with apprehenfion, " I conjure you, Rofina, to tell me the caufe of your diftrefs."

" Seek not to know the caufe of my diftrefs," replied Rofina; " it is enough to fay, that I am the moft unhappy wretch alive. Oh, that death would eafe me of my pain!"

" Oh Heaven, Rofina!" exclaimed Lydia, with alarm. " Pray explain yourfelf. What have I done to forfeit your efteem? I am your fifter, your friend, oh, hide not your forrows from me! repofe them with confidence in my bofom, and be affured——"

" Melford is a villain," interrupted Rofina, fobbing in a flood of tears. Lydia
looked

looked aghaft, and breathed in filence—" fo I alwıvs thought."

" Ah, Lydia, Lydia! how differently do we think of thofe we love!" replied Rofina. " But do not ımagine that I am the betrayed creature you feem to think me. I have been ımprudent, but, Heaven be praifed, I am ftill ınnocent, my foul ftarted with deteftation fıom his propofal. Oh, he has cruelly deceıved me! he has torn open the tendereft receffes of my heart, his treachery, however, may be of fervice; he has opened my eyes to the duplicıty of the world; he has taught me a leffon of cautıon and dıf-truft, he has, Lydıa, yes, my dear fifter, he has taught me to blufh for my paft ın-difcretıon, and made me refolve never more to yıeld a willıng ear to the deceitful tongue of flattery and adulatıon."

" Gracious

"Gracious Providence! I thank thee," cried Lydia, raifing her lovely eyes to heaven. "Thou haft preferved my fifter from a villain's wiles, the grey hairs of a parent from forrow, and my heart from breaking."

Rofina, when the agitation of her fpirits were compofed, gave a faithful narrative to her fifter of every word that had paffed, and of every incident which had ever happened between her and Melford, from his firft acquaintance to the prefent time.

The mind of Lydia was intereftedly attentive to every fentence of Rofina's narrative; and her emotions evidently difcovered that her heart was labouring with a fecret which her tongue would be unable to conceal. "Is it poffible," fhe exclaimed, as her fifter concluded, "that two characters fo extremely different as Captain Manning and

and Captain Melford; can really entertain
the warm and cordial friendſhip for each
other which they mutually profeſs? Oh Roſina! liſten to me while I diſcloſe the particulars of an event which fills my breaſt
with mingled pain and pleaſure. I might
now have been weeping with anguiſh over
the diſappointed wiſhes of a deluded heart,
but that Manning is the moſt generous of
mankind. Honour holds her ſacred throne
within his breaſt; and Virtue is the arbiter
of all his actions; he perceived the power
which his merits have ſilently gained in my
affections, but, diſdaining to take an ad-
vantage of my weakneſs, he has generouſly
cautioned me, with the warmth of a lover,
and with the ſincerity of a friend, to repreſs
the progreſs of a paſſion which particular
circumſtances, he ſays, muſt inevitably render hopeleſs. You may remember that after
we

we came home, on the evening when we were driven from the parade by the intoxication of the Officers, I was left alone with Manning in the parlour. The recollection of some expressions which he had made to me during the entertainments of the morning had agitated my spirits to a great degree, and the opportunity of privacy induced him to resume the subject. My feelings were excited beyond my strength, and I fainted away. I remained for some moments senseless; but when I recovered, I found Manning, the generous Manning, leaning over me with anxious solicitude. After a momentary silence, he exclaimed, ' Oh Lydia! I cannot describe the concern which your illness has given me. I have watched returning life with anxious expectation. Oh that I could watch for ever over you with guardian care! But, alas! the fates will not

permit

permit me to indulge that pleafing hope. I am no ftranger, Lydia, to the fituation of your heart, and I cannot reft any longer without coming to an ecclaircifTement. I admire, I love, I adore you, you are the friend of my heart, and the pride of my affections, never did I behold you without emotion. Your beauty firft gained dominion over my mind, and your ineftimable virtues have eftablifhed your fovereignty in my heart. A cruel fate, alas! forbids me to indulge a hopelefs paffion, or I fhould long ere now have made my feelings known, and have endeavoured, by every honourable expedient, to unite your deftiny with mine. A matrimonial engagement which I am under, and which honour binds me to confider as facred, as indiffoluble, as if the nuptial ceremony had already paffed, tears me from the object of my wifhes. But abfence cannot efface your image from my mind, you will be ever prefent to my view, and I fear that wretchednefs is my inevitable doom. The trial is fevere, oh! teach me, thou fair and gentle being, the virtues of patience, mildnefs, and refignation, teach me to rely upon that Power who alone can foften my forrows, and calm my agitated mind '—My tears ftreamed down my cheeks —' Ah Lydia!' continued he, ' what do thofe tears exprefs? if I have difturbed your tranquillity, my misfortunes will be great indeed. But I will fly immediately from a place in which I find I cannot, confiftently with your peace and my own honour, ftay a moment longer.'

" He then informed me of his intention to proceed directly to London. Oh Rofina! I difcovered emotions during this interview which I hope cannot be condemned as im-

prudent

prudent. fome proof of reciprocal regard
was furely due to fuch unfeigned affection.

" When we parted, ' remember me,'
faid he, ' in the light a friend. As a friend,
I hope you will never forget me. Think
of me as one anxioufly interefted for your
welfare; whofe chief, whofe only felicity,'
he added with a figh, ' muft depend upon
knowing that you are happy. The period
may in time arrive when my heart will find
peace, but at prefent we muft part, my
dear, my gentle, my generous Lydia; for
I can no longer truft to the dangerous
pleafure of beholding you.'

" Oh Rofina! we have indeed parted,
I fear, for ever; but I fhall never forget the
noble-minded Manning. It is my conftant
though fruitlefs wifh, to follow his advice,
and confider him in the light of a friend;
but the lover rifes conftantly to my view;

K 2   and

and my heart feels a comfort from the indulgence of a melancholy hope amidst the tempest of despair.

"I feel a pleasure in contemplating the virtues which have occasioned my pain, and I would not exchange the present sorrows of my heart for all the joys which a common affection, uninterrupted in its progress, could possibly bestow. This declaration might appear a paradox to those whose breasts have never known the force of love; but you, who have felt its power, will believe it to be true."

"Noble Manning!" cried Rosina, sighing at the contrast she was unavoidably obliged to draw. "Your situation, Lydia, must be happiness itself, when compared with mine. The advantages which your prudence and discretion have gained, must contribute to exalt you in your own opinion, while the

the folly and giddinefs of mine degrades me below the poffibility of comfort. Thine are the triumphs of virtue, the comforts of prudence, the applaufes of parental affection, while I"——She attempted to proceed, but a burft of forrow choaked her utterance.

While Lydia was affording her kindeft affiftance to alleviate the forrows of Rofina's mind, Mifs Margaret entered the room to acquaint them that fupper was on the table. Rofina endeavoured to excufe herfelf from going down, but her aunt would take no denial, and it was in vain to oppofe her.

The Vicar remarked the dejection of his daughter's fpirits, which he attributed to the intended departure of the regiment the next morning, nor was he quite miftaken. The youthful heart of Rofina had received its firft impreffions of love from Melford, and

thofe

those impreffions are not eafily eradicated. Notwithftanding the treatment, therefore, which fhe had received, his image ftill haunted her mind, and while fhe condemned, fhe adored him.

Rofina retired, at an early hour, to bed, but fleep had fled, with comfort, from her pillow. She paffed the long hours in reftlefs thought, until fatigue and anxiety procured her an interrupted flumber. About three o'clock in the morning the found of martial mufic ftruck her ear. She ftarted from her uneafy repofe. " They are going!" fhe cried, "Oh Lydia, they are going!" Lydia, alarmed from a found fleep, enquired what was the matter. " The regiment, the regiment is marching!" exclaimed Rofina; and flying to the window, fhe viewed them unobferved from behind the curtain.

The

The band was playing immediately before the houfe, where Meliord had contrived upon fome pretence, to halt; fondly flattering himfelf that he might poffibly fee his Rofina once again at one of the windows. He raifed his fine eyes to every part of the building, but when he found that his expectations were difappointed, his features became obfcured and gloomy, his eyes funk in profound melancholy, and he ordered the foldiers to proceed on their march. Rofina ftood liftening to the beat of the drum until it founded in her ear like a diftant echo; and then, burfting into a flood of tears, returned to a bed of forrow and defpair. "Cruel Melford!" fhe exclaimed, as fhe placed her head upon the pillow, "how could you ingratiate yourfelf into my bofom with no other view than to torture my heart? But your treachery has taught me wifdom;

K 4 and

and may hereafter be of fervice." But when fhe looked to that *hereafter* without the fociety of Melford, without even the profpect of ever feeing him again, it only aggravated her difcontent.

The family were fummoned to breakfaft at the ufual time the next morning. The regiment was gone, and the Vicar was in excellent fpirits. "I can now, methinks," faid he, "look around me with fecurity, but while thofe doughty heroes infefted the place, I was in hourly expectation of having my little caftle ftormed, and my treafures carried away." He obferved the fwoln eyes of Rofina; a circumftance of which he thought it improper to take notice; but he endeavoured to rally both his daughters into good fpirits, for the breaft of Lydia, befides her own forrows, ever felt a portion of Rofina's diftrefs.

The

The Vicar, to divert their minds, promifed to walk with them in the evening to
a delightful fpot in the neighbourhood,
which he had by accident found out, and
to introduce them to a ftranger who, he faid,
expected their company to tea.

There was a myfterious novelty in this
propofal which excited their curiofity, and
to which they inftantly acceded. Mifs Margaret was as impatient as her nieces to learn
who this ftranger could poffibly be. After
dinner, therefore, they equipped themfelves
for walking, and having proceeded about
two miles, they ftruck into a narrow road,
where they never before had been. At the
extremity of this road they croffed the cor-
ner of a wild and unfrequented heath, and,
arriving at the entrance of a wood, the Vicar
opened a fmall gate, which he informed
them led to the ftranger's habitation.

K 5   CHAP.

———————

CHAP. XIII.

THE STORY OF MELINDA.

IN a fmall glen ftood a cottage, the fit abode of folitude, melancholy, and con-templation. Straggling rows of poplars caft a deep fhade on the cafement; around which the hand of time had planted little fprouts of ivy. A channel, muddy, winding, and contracted, flowed through the bottom, un-difturbed by a murmur, unruffled by a curl. Willows, properly called weeping, inter-

fperfed

sperfed with a few flowers the spontaneous growth of nature, covered its banks, and gave an aspect of gloomy wildness to all around.

Mr. Ouseley's companions were struck with awe and admiration at the silent solemnity of the scene. They contemplated every part with deep attention, no human object was to be seen, all was still, calm, motionless, and their hearts felt congenial sorrow from the impressive gloominess they surveyed. The Vicar, at length, unlatched the cottage door, and conducted them into a room where sat the melancholy mistress of this lonely shade. On beholding her, a sudden emotion thrilled through the nerves of her trembling visitors. The pathetic words of Lady Randolph were truly descriptive of her appearance:—

"Is

" In

K 6

" In me thou doſt behold

" The poor remains of beauty, once admired,

" The autumn of my days is come already,

" For ſorrow made my ſummer haſte away "

DOUGLAS

She was indeed in the autumn of her days, but the golden harveſt of ſerenity and joy which ſhould have attended it, ſeemed to be fatally blighted by affliction. The baleful effects of calamity were eaſily to be traced on every fine and expreſſive feature of her face. Her perſon, by nature elegant and graceful, was worn down with the ravages of ſorrow. A belt of ſtraw, curiouſly interwoven, confined a white garment round her waiſt, a hat, formed of the ſame materials, was tied on her head, in a ruſtic manner, with a green ribbon, part of her hair, which was of a dark colour, was faſtened in a braid with a ſmall comb, the

5

other

other part hung negligent and difordered, in great length, upon her fhoulders; but fo commanding is real lovelinefs, that even in this attire fhe impreffed the minds of her vifitors with refpect and admiration.

"According to my promife," faid the Vicar, "I have brought my young pupils to vifit you; they are good and harmlefs; let me requeft for them your friendly ad- monitions."

"The office of a monitor," replied the lady, "I accept with pleafure. To warn others, by my example, to avoid the dan- gerous precipice from which I have fatally fallen, is perhaps the only focial duty that is now left me to perform; and the profpect of doing good will more than compenfate for the pain I may feel in relating the forrows of my heart."

A little

A little rosy girl, the picture of health, and the emb'em of innocence, brought in an humble equipage of tea, with some country bifcuits, and fmall pats of butter. A converfation upon indifferent fubjects enfued; which introduced the ladies to greater eafe and familiarity with each other. When the fimple repaft was finifhed, Mr. Oufeley and his family drew their chairs round that of their melancholy entertainer; who, like the good Genii inftructing unfufpecting youth, began as follows:—

"The tale of real woe does not require the aid of ornament to affect the heart. Truth is great and powerful: I fhall not, therefore, attempt to ufe the fictitious imagery of the novelift, in relating to you the painful ftory of my life.

"My

"My name is Melinda Clifford: my father was an Enfign: in his fecond engagement he received a wound which totally difabled him, and he was obliged to retire from the fervice with no means of fupport but his half-pay, and with no treafure but his honour and myfelf. My mother died foon after I was born, and all the warmth of affection which he entertained for her, he transferred to me. To fay that he loved me with parental tendernefs, would not be doing juftice to the force of his affection. His life, his foul, were wrapped up in mine; and if one human being ever idolized another, that being was my father. We chofe as the place of our abode, a cottage in a fequeftered part of Carnarvonfhire, whofe humble roof was fuited to the abject ftate of our finances: here we were literally

"Almoft

"; Almoſt on Nature's common bounty fed;

" Like the gay birds that ſung us to repoſe,

" Content and careleſs of to-morrow's fare"

THOMSON.

" Until I attained the age of eighteen all was ſerenity and humble peace. A native cheerfulneſs of diſpoſition prevented the dread of worldly want from preying long upon my mind; and the careſſes of my fond father baniſhed the recollection of thoſe little cares which would now and then obtrude themſelves upon my repoſe. The anxieties of his mind upon my account, when he recollected the precarious nature of his ſituation, were, I am convinced, great and piercing, but his tenderneſs induced him to conceal from me the troubles of his heart. The ſorrowful reflection, that upon his death, he muſt leave his darling child to the mercy of a harſh world, with-

out

out fortune and without a friend, prompted the hope, that the perfections which he flattered himself I poffeffed, would afford him the opportunity of feeing me foon advantageoufly fettled in the world; and he refolved to concur with the firft honourable offer that I fhould receive.

"At this period the fon of a neighbouring farmer honoured me with his addreffes; but my foolifh heart rejected his advances; and I could never prevail upon myfelf to let him apply to his parents for their confent. My father, ever anxious to cultivate the talents with which nature had endowed me, had created in my mind an ardent fondnefs for the elegant occupation of reading. Books were my great delight, and my foul caught from them an idea of refinement incompatible with the lowlinefs of my ftation. My foul was alive to all the fenfibilities of tendernefs;

tendernefs, my mind dwelt with rapture on
the purities of love, I was the complete
pupil of romance. From reciprocal delicacy of fentiment my heart expected to
derive its higheft pleafures; but my lover
appeared to be devoid of all tafte, and I
could fcarcely fupport myfelf under the idea
of becoming the wife of fuch a being. I
fighed at the cruel deftiny which would doom
me to a perfon whom I confidered as barely
human; but my father preffed me to encourage his hopes, and to gratify the wifhes
of my father, I refolved to conquer my
reluctance, and promote his eafe, by the
facrifice of my own.

" While I was endeavouring to fublue
the afpiring notions which I had imbibed,
and to reduce my fentiments to a level with
my fituation, an accident happened which
proved fatal to cur repofe.

" Our

" Our humble habitation adjoined a haggard belonging to a neighbouring farmer. The hay in it took fire; the rapidity of the flames baffled the timid and awkward exertions of the peafants to extinguifh them, and communicating deftruction to our only home, confumed in a moment every thing we poffeffed. The fudden lofs of all our property plunged us at once into the depths of mifery; but the dreadful condition to which it reduced my poor father, fuperfeded every other confideration in my mind than that which was immediately neceffary to the fafety of his life. It affected his fenfes, and he was borne the helplefs victim of calamity to an adjacent hut; where, after fome perfuafion, the wretched owner permitted us to ftay.

" My lover was unfortunately abfent from the country, and, as his addreffes to me

were

'were unknown to his family, we could derive no affiftance from that quarter; and we not knew whither to turn for fupport.

" One morning, while I was weeping with diftraction over that being whofe exiftence I held far dearer than my own, and whofe emaciated and languifhing body feemed to implore the affiftance which I had not the power to procure him, an unknown perfon came to our wretched habitation, and delivered me a purfe containing twenty guineas, faying, as he departed, that it came from a gentleman who had heard of, and pitied our misfortunes. Frantic with joy, as I had before been with grief, I devoutly thanked the Providence who had fo unexpectedly fent us this relief. My grateful heart poured out unnumbered bleffings on the head of our generous and unknown benefactor; and I bufied myfelf,

with

with rapture, in providing nouriſhment for my almoſt exhauſted and expiring parent.

" The meſſenger who had delivered me the purſe came regularly every morning with enquiries after our health, loaded with ſuch delicacies as were particularly calculated to reſtore the health of an invalid. We preſſed him continually to make us acquainted with the name and ſituation of our worthy and munificent benefactor; and, after repeated entreaty, he, at length, informed us that his maſter only waited for our permiſſion to pay us a viſit. The delicacy of ſentiment which this heſitation implied, was congenial to the ruling paſſion of my ſoul; and expreſſing the gratitude of our hearts, we mentioned the next morning to receive our benefactor.——

" He came.——

" Oh,

" Oh, had he never come! Had he continued to perform the offices of benevolence
concealed and unknown, I fhould have confidered him as the pureft minifter of humanity, and, as fuch, have adored him: youth,
beauty, elegance, infinuation, every natural,
every acquired, every beguiling grace
adorned him. Already taught to confider
him as the preferver of our exiftence, awe,
refpect, love, and admiration thrilled tu-
multuoufly through my veins at his approach,
and my heart fell a victim to its gratitude.

" I was a ftranger to guile, and ignorant of
the duplicity of the world, but nature bade
every feeling of my foul to glow with the
warmeft tranfport towards a man who had fo
generoufly raifed us from the abyfs of mifery
and defpair. The poor and lowly hut in
which we lodged was, he faid, ill fuited to
the merit of its inmates, and he eafily per-

fuaded

fuaded us to remove to a houfe neat, commodious, and delightfully fituated to pleafe a romantic mind, which he provided for our reception.

"My humble lover ftill peftered me with his addreffes; but I turned from them with difguft. My creative mind had opened profpects to my view, which gratified the ambition of my foul. Even my poor deluded parent no longer pleaded in his favour. He, like myfelf, fondly imagined that our liberal benefactor looked with tranfports of the pureft love on Melinda, and thought of exalting her to his own fphere. My paffion increafed, but it was not birth, it was not fortune which added fuel to the flame; it was a paffion kindled by a contemplation of the angelic virtues which I imagined he poffeffed; and with him ficknefs, forrow, folitude, would have been, to my mind,

health,

health, happineſs, and ſociety. Love, once admitted, ſteals ſilently and unperceived through all the devious labyrinths of the heart. He obſerved the aſcendancy which his aſſumed virtues gained over my warm, thankful, unſuſpecting breaſt, and he ſeized a favourable opportunity to reveal his deſigns. A tender, artleſs, inexperienced girl, I ſaw not the errors into which my miſguided mind was leading me——but I will not attempt to palliate my tranſgreſſion. When the man on whom my heart had long reſted in perfect confidence of happineſs wept over me with agonizing tenderneſs, Virtue, at a fatal moment, forſook her charge, and I conſented to forſake my parent.

" Oh, miſerable veteran in calamity! how often has the pinching hand of poverty afflicted thee! how often haſt thou looked

up

up exultingly, and fmiled with kindnefs on thy child!

" Villain! fpecious villain! beneath the cloak of compaffion to meditate a blow fo dire, fo abhorred, fo inhuman! to tear from the bofom of the aged parent his laft, his only fupport, and crufh at once two miferable victims!

," My feducer conveyed me from the bowers of fecurity and content to the regions of diffipation and extravagance; but the noify tumults of giddy pleafure had no power over the more tumultuous reproaches of my inward monitor. Pleafure appeared to my mind ftretched on the rack. Gay fmiling innocence, the foothing cherub which gilded fterile penury, and made content a conftant gueft at the ftinted board, was irretrievably gone. The moft fplendid profufion could furnifh no charms to pleafe

me: prodigality could purchase no ornament
to delight my mind or ease my heart. I
passed two years in a state of misery which
the slaves who dig in the entrails of Gol-
conda, those wretched tools of avarice and
ambition, would have pitied. The being
at whose absence my mind was used to pine
and sicken, at whose presence my heart was
used to beat with renovated pleasure, became odious to my recollection. The idea
of an injured father haunted me perpetually,
and, in a moment of madness and despair,
I tore from my hated form the gaudy trap-
pings of vice, and precipitately fled from
my betrayer's house.

"The hope of being received into my
father's arms again, of closing my eyes upon
his fond bosom, of mingling his blessings
with my expiring sighs, cheered my des-
ponding heart, and directed my trembling

steps

steps towards his habitation. It was then near the conclusion of the autumn, and the darkness of the evening had closed in as my wearied feet, reached the place of his abode. Chill horror thrilled through all my veins as I surveyed the house. The windows were all barred, nettles covered the threshold of the door, and the dreary look of desolation which surrounded it, proclaimed that its inhabitant was gone. Every circumstance of former happiness, which I had enjoyed under its roof, rushed cruelly to my mind: I wrung my hands, I tore my dishevelled hair, I acted like what I was—a lunatic.

'Oh!' I exclaimed, as I lay upon the earth, ' that I was deep, deep interred! that the sod which covers the most injured of men pressed on my cold breast, a wretch! a wanderer! a fugitive! oh sacred spirit of my much-injured parent, look down, look down upon the creature who was once thy favourite child! cancel her misdeeds with an angel's forgiveness, and pray that death may soon release her from her troubles!

"While I was thus bewailing the sad consequences of my fatal misconduct, a violent storm of rain, accompanied by universal darkness, overspread the hemisphere, and filled me with horror   I wandered for some time not knowing where I went.   At length, I discovered a glimmering light beaming from a distant hovel, I crept towards it as well as I was able, and tapped at the door.   An old woman, the only object visible, opened it, and afforded me a shelter from the inclement night.   So woeworn a figure as my form presented to her sight, she had never before beheld.   The tears of pity trickled down the furrows of her

her aged cheek; and perceiving my diſtreſs
and fatigue, ſhe kindly invited me to ſhare
her pallet of ſtraw. - She brought me ſome
homely food, but nature, worn out by grief
and faſting, loathed all nutriment, and ſhe
could only prevail with me to moiſten my
parched lips with a little milk, warmed over
the expiring embers of a fire. I laid my
aching head upon the ſtraw, in hopes of
reſt. The fatigue I had undergone kindly
cloſed my eyes, but torturing fancy continued to diſturb my mind with images of
horror. I awoke ſeveral times ſcarcely able
to breathe, with a dew, cold as the icicles
of death, upon my forehead.

"While I lay diſordered and reſtleſs, a
groan penetrated my ear, another followed
which pierced me to the ſoul. I ſtarted in
an agony, and waking the old woman, who
lay ſnoring by my ſide, enquired from whence

L 3 the

the founds proceeded. She informed me that a poor old man, who had for fome fhort time lodged in an inner room of her hut, was extremely ill, and expected to die. I afked her if he had any one with him to alleviate the deep pain he feemed to feel. She was about to anfwer; when the found of a voce, which will ever remain unobliterated upon my memory, ftruck my fenfe, and thrilled through every vein of my body. I rufhed into the room, which was only a poor fhed, feparated from that in which I lay by a rude partition, and on a heap of ftraw I difcovered the dying father of Melinda! a half extinguifhed candle caft a dreary gleam of light acrofs the room. The winds whiftled through the crevices of the hovel. His reftlefs head feemed as if it was endeavouring to conceal itfelf from the cold and chilling blaft. He was calling for drink.

‘ All-

' All gracious Power!' I cried, ' is this my parent? Oh, what,' I sighed, wringing my hands, ' are all the sorrows I have felt to this? ·this is real woe; it leads to madness:—Oh! Oh!—Oh! my parent! friend! darling! solace of my heart!'—I pressed his livid lips, cold with the icy hand of hastening death.— He knew me—but what passed I was for some time deprived of knowing.

" When I recovered from my swoon, I found the old woman supporting me in her lap. My father, who had vainly attempted to rise, was regarding me with unutterable agonies. The scene that followed is too dreadful to relate, language could not paint it, and indeed my senses were so disordered, that I myself remain happily ignorant of almost all that passed. Amidst the pangs of dissolution he caressed, blessed, and pardoned me. He faintly cried, ' Oh, vice!

who

how horrid are thy depredations! haplefs
Melinda, its fated victim! my child, thy
form befpeaks thy penitence. The rofes
of thy youth are faded, the fmile of gaiety
is flown; the luftre of thine eyes is extinguifhed by defpair. May thy contrition
render thee fit for that heaven which can
now be thy only refource for comfort! if you
fhould furvive your forrows, may you with
humility warn others by your example!
But oh! when you mention your fufferings,
mention alfo the folly of your parent. Bid
other fathers beware of the ruin he has occafioned to his child, and teach them not
to place their children within the reach of
danger, by idle expectations of advancement
and ambition.'

   " On my bofom his forgiving, pure, and
fond fpirit fled from forrow, want, and difeafe, to the manfions of the dead."

                              Melinda

Melinda endeavoured to proceed in the sequel of her story, but a burst of tears stopped her utterance. She rose suddenly from her chair to indulge the sensibility of her heart. For some time she was unable to proceed; but she, at length, conquered her sorrow, and continued in broken accents.

"My betrayer had received immediate intelligence of my flight. Stung by remorse at the treachery he had committed, he pursued me, and, at this awful moment, discovering my retreat, dared to break in once more upon the privilege of wretchedness. When he beheld me, my haggard looks betrayed evident marks of approaching mortality. Guilt shook his soul to its inmost recesses, and all the wrongs of injured innocence rose dreadful to his view. He sighed, he fell prostrate at my feet; he groaned forth his sorrow; and offered to

L 5 repair

repair the violence he had committed by making me his wife.

'Villain!' I cried indignantly, 'doſt thou imagine that either thy hand or thy fortune can make reparation for the injuries I have received? can thy grief, thy penitence, re-animate the dead? can the pollution of in-famy be waſhed away by remorſe? when I conſidered you a man of virtue, I loved, I adored you. The wide world has not a woe in it that I would not have patiently borne for your ſake, but my ſoul now turns from you with abhorrence. You are the betrayer of my happineſs and your own honour. Look, look on that pale corpſe, the victim of our crimes! Oh, think how you have converted his bleſſing into a curſe, and rendered his daughter his executioner!'

" He obſerved every nerve of my feeble frame ſtrained with agony; he ſaw my eyes

fix

fix within their burning fockets, he faw the figns of rifing frenzy in my countenance; and he knew—oh terrible!—he knew himfelf to be my deftroyer. The tribunal at which he muft one day anfwer for his crimes rufhed to his imagination, and he fell in agony to the ground.

" Did his fighs gratify my ears? no; I was not fanguinary or vindictive; but I acknowledge that I felt a luxury while I bent in fympathizing pity over the man who had ftolen my virgin affections.

" My undoer was now proftrate, a penitent and humble wretch, at my feet. My mind was unequal to the feverity of my contending paffions. My fenfes failed; and I continued for two years infenfible to my woe.

" My lover, as I have fince been informed, ordered the remains of my poor

father

father to be carried to the grave in decent funeral. He attended the obsequies himself, and raised a monument of his own repentance by the tributary tears which he shed upon the grave. The old woman, whose hospitable hut had given a temporary shelter to our miseries, was taken by his grateful munificence from her state of indigence, and placed among the cottagers of his own estate. Tortured by a retrospection of his past conduct, and anxious to make every atonement in his power for the miseries he had entailed upon me, I was carefully removed to an apartment in his own house, where every endeavour was exerted to administer comfort to a mind diseased. I was guarded with the tenderest care, soothed by unremitted kindness, and all my wanderings indulged.

"But

"But even the obliterating effect of madness could not erase from my mind the direful remembrance that he was the contriver of all my miseries; and upon the return of my reason, I peremptorily insisted on departing from his house. He endeavoured to convert my resolution by every argument ingenuity could suggest, he entreated me to stay, with all the warmth of unaffected love, and with all the humility of sincere repentance, but I was inexorable to his prayers. The exertions of my industry I conceived would procure me support; and my soul rose indignant at the idea of receiving accommodation or relief from the man who had abused the sacred names of friendship and benevolence, for the purpose of corrupting my virtue. The spirit of my dear and injured father rose before my view, and inspired my mind with an invincible antipathy

to

to my betrayer. I vowed with all the per-
tinacity of an unalterable refolution, never
to fee him more, and, as he dreaded that
a return of madnefs might be the confequence of reiterated oppofition, he, at
length, relinquifhed his fruitlefs endeavours
to detain me; and I abandoned his habitation, friendlefs and forlorn. The fcene
of his paft happinefs became odious to himfelf, and I have been fince informed that
he alfo foon after quitted his houfe, and now
lives abroad, a wretched exile from his native
country and his friends, a prey to confuming
forrow and remorfe. A lady who had heard
my tale took me under her roof, cherifhed,
and protected me, and at her death, which
happened foon afterwards, made ample pro-
vifion for my future comfort. While my
foul was languifhing for folitude, I difcovered
this retreat, where I have now lived ten

years,

years, and where I hope to breathe my laft. Your father in an accidental walk overheard me venting my complaints. He introduced himfelf to my notice, and by his frequent vifits, and confolatory precepts, has, in fome degree, calmed the perturbation of my mind. At my requeft he folemnly pro-mifed not to difcover the place of my re-treat, nor even to mention my exiftence, till time and the influence of thofe religious devotions which he has inculcated, had foft-ened the keennefs of my forrows. He lately expreffed a defire that you fhould hear my ftory: I wifhed to oblige him, and, re-membering the dying words of my beloved parent, to teach others wifdom by my folly, I no longer refufed to comply with his requeft.

" May my tale make the impreffion that I wifh! May innocence learn from it to

beware

beware of the beguiling tongue of flattery!
May it alfo learn that even gratitude, the
fweeteft emotion of the heart, may, by
opening the avenues of tendernefs, while it
lulls the vigilance of fufpicion, lead to confequences fatal to our repofe!—Oh, ye
daughters of purity, liften to the fad moni-
trefs of forrow! Fly! fly! from the de-
lufive tale of the flagitious, and be affured
that when prudence fuffers any inroad, virtue verges to a decline."

So fpoke Melinda Clifford, and her voice
breathed the fentiments of her amanuenfis,
who hopes, when thofe eyes which now
wander over their own pages are clofed in
death, when the fibres of that hand which
now writes them are unftrung, this humble
tale

tale will gain, if not approbation, at leaſt the paſſing tribute of a ſigh for the memory of one who was, if not an uſeful, a harmleſs member of ſociety.

CHAP. XIV.

THE EFFECT OF EXAMPLE.

THE hearts of Lydia and Roſina were too ſuſceptible of tenderneſs not to deeply ſympathize in the melancholy narrative of Melinda's life. Miſs Margaret, who was

particularly

particularly fond of all that was romantic and pathetic, shed many tears, and loudly inveighed against the perfidy of man.

Rosina, sighing, reflected, with sadness, on the similitude she was compelled to draw between Melford and Melinda's betrayer. When her past conduct, her levity, her wildness presented themselves to her view, she was shocked and ashamed; conscious that she was obliged to Providence alone for the preservation of that honour, which she had, by an egregious love of admiration, so imprudently laid snares to betray.

Lydia, while she commiserated the misfortunes she had heard related, felt her bosom warm with a triumphant glow, at the remembrance of her Manning's virtues.

The reason why the Vicar was so anxious for them to hear the particulars of Melinda's story was now obvious to their minds, and this

this difcovery, perhaps, in fome meafure leff-
ened its effect.

"In this folitude," faid Mifs Clifford,
"I enjoy a calm which I once imagined I
fhould never again experience. Religion,
retirement, and the arguments of my worthy
friend your father, have given unexpected
tranquillity to my mind. Books, work, and
contemplation principally engrofs my time.
I cultivate no acquaintance but with the
neighbouring peafants, whofe little wants,
as far as it is in my power, I endeavour
to relieve. My chief companion is the
young girl whom you faw wait at tea. She
is grand-daughter to the poor woman who
kindly fheltered my unhappy parent. Juftice
and gratitude, as well as humanity, called
upon me to protect the friendlefs innocence
of an orphan from the dangerous inclemency
of an unfeeling world. I now and then

recreate

recreate my fpirits by liftening with admiration to the artlefs tale of blufhing fimplicity.   A life fpent like mine, may appear horrid and gloomy to thofe who have never felt adver-fity.   But ah, my young friends! fuch a fituation as I am now in, is to me like the verdure of green fhades, and the refrefhing coolnefs of ftreams to the traveller, fcorched by the peftilential heat of burning fands."

Melinda invited her vifitors to walk round her little retreat, and they accepted the invitation with pleafure.   On their firft entrance, they had confidered it as the gloomy recefs of horror and defpair, but they now viewed it as the bower of hope, and the retreat of content, and fancy gave to every object a new appearance.

There was a beauty in its parts which had efcaped their obfervation.   The dark labyrinths of the wood were changed to

pleafing

pleafing groves. The drooping boughs of
the willow, inftead of being emblems of
forrow, were ftriving with eagernefs to kifs
the ftream. The muddy channel was converted into a purling rill. Flowers of beauty
and of fragrance fprang beneath their feet,
and woodbines flaunted, with gay luxuriance,
upon every tree. Unconfcious that the
change was owing to the different temper
of their minds, they were aftonifhed at the
different complexion which every object
affumed. Rofina thought it the feat of
happinefs The love-fick foul of Lydia
languifhed for its privacy, and Mifs Margaret faid, it was finely adapted for the enjoyment of philofophic fpeculation.

The mild radiance of the moon began to
gild the tops of fome lofty pines which
adorned the fummit of an adjacent hill, the
blue expanfe of the fky was all befpangled
with

with the brighteſt ſtars. Melinda, caſting her
eyes to heaven, "Thoſe glittering harbingers
of night," ſaid ſhe, " often employ my mind,
I envy thoſe who underſtand aſtronomy, it
is a ſtudy which muſt ennoble, purify, and
ſublime our ideas.   How delightful muſt it
be to contemplate, with a perfect knowledge
of their nature, the wonderful works of the
Great Creator! Increaſing admiration, gratitude, and praiſe muſt follow, when we
I now the various purpoſes for which theſe
bright appearances are ordained,—

" Even thy loweſt works, yet theſe dec――
" Thy goodneſs beyond thought, and pow'r divine.
" Speak, ye who beſt can tell, ye ſons of light,
" Angels, for ye behold him, and with ſongs,
" And choral ſymphonies, day without night,
" Circle his throne rejoicing   Ye in heaven,
" On earth, join all ye creatures to extol
" Him firſt, Him laſt, Him midſt, and without end."

MILTON

She

She recited this beautiful paffage with a voice fo clear, fo fweet, fo affecting, with a look of piety fo finely adapted to its fenfe, as plainly evinced that confolations of religion had infpired her mind with perfect refignation, and prepared her to meet, without difmay, the great and awful mandate of Almighty power.

The Vicar reminded his companions of the latenefs of the hour, and the length of the walk which they had to take. Melinda obtained a promife from the ladies to renew their vifits, and they parted from each other with great reluctance, and mutual careffes.

The ftory of Melinda's misfortunes, and the amiable character fhe appeared to poffefs, naturally became the fubject of their converfation as they walked ho ne.

"You

" You hear, my beloved children," faid the Vicar, " the fatal confequences which refult from inconfiderate credulity. The imprudencies to which it leads make ruin inevitable, and, I had almoft faid, deferved. You fee the dangerous folly of encouraging ambitious hopes, and looking to connections beyond the fphere in which we move. Had the mifguided Clifford given his daughter to the worthy farmer, had he not liftened to the flattering hope of raifing her to fuperior rank, they might ftill have been happy."

" And yet, papa," faid Rofina, " we frequently hear of handfome girls being married to great fortunes, and fometimes to titles, on account of their beauty."

" True, my child," replied the Vicar, " inftances of this kind may happen, but not fo frequently as fame reports, and to raife

the

the expectations of hope beyond a rational probability of gratification, always opens a source of difappointment, vexation, and danger."

"Nonfenfe, brother!" cried Mifs Margaret, "you ftrive to extinguifh all ambition from the girls' breafts. I fay they fhould always look above their own fphere. They fhould always encourage an expectation of the moft fplendid alliances. Don't tell me of dangers and difappointments, and vexations, there is much more danger to be apprehended from a mean and grovelling mind, than from a high fpirit, and afpiring notions. If I were a Queen, I would not be content. I would ftill endeavour to foar above my fphere."

The Vicar was not very well pleafed with his fifter's fentiments upon this fubject; but knowing that the more he oppofed them,

the

the more her violence would increase, he endeavoured to ftop the further propagation of her fchifms, by changing the fubject of converfation.

On their arrival at the Vicarage they found the cloth ready fpread for fupper, to which they immediately fat down. The Vicar refumed his natural good fpirits, and in a vein of raillery, which Mifs Margaret could not controvert, entirely overturned her airy fyftem of promoting the ends of happinefs by endangering the interefts of virtue. It was a fubject in which the future conduct of his daughters was deeply concerned; and as he had, by a few fuccefsful obfervations, entirely filenced his fifter's oppofition, he continued to inculcate the advantages of prudence and humility, till the found of a carriage ftopping at the door put an end to his converfation. Rofina

turned

turned pale; the idea of Melford returning in the character of a penitent lover was uppermost in her thoughts. What Lydia felt we cannot ascertain; she rose, reseated herself upon a chair, and trembled exceedingly. The Vicar went out to see who it was that could come to him at so extraordinary an hour; and curiosity induced the girls to follow him.

CHAP.

CHAP. XV.

A DUEL.

THE moment the door was opened, a gentleman alighted from the carriage, and affisted by a fervant, bore into the hall the body of a man apparently breathlefs, whofe clothes were ftained with the vital ftream of life.

The Vicar, like the good Samaritan, concluded that it was fome unfortunate traveller, who, as he journeyed on his way had

had fallen among thieves, and been barbarously ufed. He approached to bind up his wounds; to afford him every humane affiftance, and to offer him an afylum in his manfion of peace. With a heart expanding to benevolence the good man was proffering his fervices. But at that inftant, almoft every fenfe fled! for beneath the afpect of immediate death, he difcovered the features of his fon, his darling fon Francis! A groan of the deepeft forrow broke from his heart. "Oh my child! my child!" he exclaimed, "who has done this? my boy, fond darling of my hopes! Oh my fon! my fon! Oh, that I could die for thee my lovely Francis!" The girls, almoft infenfible of their exiftence, hung round their parent, with inarticulate forrow.

When the firft burft of grief was over, the confternation and horror which the lad

fcene

scene had occasioned, gave way to anxiety for the poor-sufferer. He was conveyed to bed; and the apothecary, whom Susan had instinctively fetched from the village on hearing that it was the body of her young master, amidst this distracted and doting family, dressed a wound, the pain of which, joined to the fatigue of travelling, had rendered Francis totally senseless. The apothecary gave no hopes of his recovery; and intimating the approach of a violent fever, desired that he might be kept undisturbed and quiet.

The stranger who had taken care of Francis, was requested to walk into the parlour; and the Vicar expressing great anxiety to be immediately informed of the cause of the disaster, he instantly complied.

"I am inexpressibly shocked, Sir," he began, "at this melancholy event; and most sincerely

sincerely commiserate the grief with which it unavoidably afflicts you. Should the consequences of it prove fatal, which Heaven in its kindness I hope will avert, it may perhaps be a sad consolation for you to be informed that your loss will be universally regretted; for the worth, genius, and spirit of your son made every one who knew him his friend; but I trust that his promising talents will be continued to a family who cannot but adore him. It is now, Sir, vacation time at the University, and he intended to surprise you agreeably by an unexpected visit. I am also a student of the same College with him; and we were equally pleased with the prospect of having the company of each other in crossing the Tweed. This morning we stopped at Earlswood to breakfast, where a regiment had halted the preceding evening."

At

At the mention of this circumſtance Roſina changed colour.

"I was unfortunately acquainted with ſome of the Officers, and we were invited to breakfaſt with them. I was ſorry to find ſtrong liquors on the tea-table, which they mixed in great abundance with their tea, I ſhall not recount the particulars of the converſation; it would indeed be here improper. A Captain Melford taking a glaſs of brandy, drank it off to the health of Miſs Ouſeley."

Roſina's chair ſhook under her, from the agitation into which the mention of Melford's name upon ſuch an occaſion naturally threw her.

"Your ſon ſtarted at the ſound, and repeated the name. Some explanations enſued, in which he found it was his ſiſter. Offended at her name being introduced in ſuch a manner, he expreſſed himſelf with ſome warmth;

warmth; there were liberties indeed taken
with her name which no brother could avoid
resenting. Words grew high, but the Officers interfered, and hoftilities were for the
prefent fufpended, but their rage was more
violent for being fmothered. They took
an opportunity to retire unobferved, without caufing the leaft fufpicion; and while
I was engaged in private converfation with
my friend, the waiter, pale and terrified,
entered the room, and informed us that one
of the gentlemen was killed. I rufhed to
the fpot where he faid they had fought;
found your fon lying on the ground; and
Captain Melford, wounded, ftanding by
him with evident concern; I procured affiftance, and had him brought to the inn. He
fuffered a furgeon to bind up his wound; but
he refufed to be put to bed, and peremptorily infifted on coming hither, that he

might,

might, if he expired, have the satisfaction of dying in the arms of his family. I thought his resolution imprudent and dangerous, and I opposed it for some time, but he remained inflexible, and till the last five miles he bore his journey with great fortitude. Captain Melford, with a distress which greatly abated my resentment towards him, before we set out, bitterly regretted the effect which his rashness had produced. You are going, said he to me, to a family whom I know and esteem, but whose domestic felicity I have by this accident unfortunately broken. It was I who gave the provocation, it was I who irritated a brother to defend the character of his sister; I alone am culpable, the affliction into which I am conscious this sad event will involve his family, overwhelms me with the keenest remorse, I have ever detested this barbarous practice;

practice;—but it is in vain to apologize for my conduct. You know that I am com- pelled to accompany my regiment to Swanf- grove, where we are to be quartered. At that place I shall be found; and should the young gentleman fall a victim to my im- petuosity, I must abide the consequences. Whenever it shall be found necessary, I shall voluntarily resign myself to the laws of my country; and although I am conscious they cannot find me guilty of premeditated malice, I fear that my own conscience will upbraid me with wantonness and intemper- ance, and peace will for ever be an alien to my heart."

Rosina, whose senses had been gradually fleeting, now fell senseless to the ground. She was carried, in convulsive agitations, to her apartment. The friend of Francis, perceiving the disorder and commotions of

the

the family, very confiderately refufed to accept the offer of a bed, and immediately
departed to his family, who refided in the
fame county, at fome diftance from the
Vicarage.

The prefent melancholy ftate of Mr.
Oufeley's family exemplifies the fatal confequences of imprudence. Rofina, by coquetry, levity, and folly, had raifed illufions
in the mind of Melford, which her unexpected virtue had fuddenly difpelled. Difappointment had foured his temper, divided
between love and ambition, half glad, half
forry, that he had not honourably purfued
his defigns, he was in that irritable frame of
mind which takes fire at the flighteft oppofition, and it now blazed forth, inflamed
with fury, on the head of the innocent but
impetuous Francis, who, folicitous for the
honour,

honour, and anxious for the welfare of his sister, could not bear to hear her name made the laugh of riot and intemperance.

––––––––––

CHAP XVI.

PARENTAL TENDERNESS.

By proper applications Rosina, at length, opened her eyes, and languidly raising them, breathed a deep sigh. "Never," she exclaimed, "shall I recover from the shock that I have received! Had my folly recoiled only upon my own head, I could have borne

it;

it; but to be the deſtroyer of my brother, my Francis, my darling brother! Oh! can my father ever bear me again in his ſight? To rob him of the comfort of his widowed days! Oh, Lydia! is there in human nature a miſery ſo intolerable as mine?"

"My deareſt love," cried her aunt, while ſhe wept over her, "compoſe your ſpirits, your brother may recover, at leaſt, your father cannot be diſpleaſed with you for an accident which you could not poſſibly occaſion."

"Ah no!" ſhe replied, "he will deteſt, abhor, abjure me, I ſhall be odious to my family and hateful to myſelf."—In uttering theſe words ſhe relapſed into the moſt violent convulſions. Her aunt terrified at the ſight of her diſtorted frame, folded her to her breaſt. Lydia flew down ſtairs to ſeek her

father,

father, and to befeech him to go up and confole the miferies of her fifter.

Cold horror oppreffed Rofina when fhe reflected that by indifcreetly fuffering fuch familiarity to Melford, fhe had been acceffary to her brother's fate; and when fhe recollected that the man whom fhe paffionately loved, in fpite of all that had happened, was in danger of his life, if, the wound fhould prove mortal, from the laws of his country, fhe gave herfelf up to violence and defpair.

Lydia overcome by conflicting emotions, funk upon a chair as fhe entered the parlour. Her tongue refufed to perform the benevolent purpofes of her heart, and her endeavours to make known the melancholy condition of her fifter were loft in inarticulate founds, till tears, like dew-drops which hang upon the drooping bell of the lily, relieved

relieved her diſtreſs. The Vicar, who had been vainly endeavouring to tranquillize his own mind, preſſed her in his arms, and mingled his tears with her's.

"Alas! my child," ſaid he, "I fear my cloudleſs day is gone for ever. My evening ſun I ſee muſt ſet in dark affliction. I fondly hoped to end a long and grievous pilgrimage, like the good old Patriarch, amidſt my children, but my boy, my darling boy, whoſe genius promiſed ſuch harveſt of felicity, is cut off in the ſummer of his days by the hand of violence. He has, however, acquired ſome reputation; and it is an alleviation of my miſery to reflect, that though death has prematurely plucked my faireſt flower, it has been ſuffered to attain ſome degree of fragrance and perfection."

"Oh, my dear father!" cried Lydia, "thoſe virtues from which you are deriving

conſolation,

confolation, will furely render his lofs more grievous and infupportable. Ah, my Francis! when I look back upon your boyifh days, when I retrace your guilelefs fports, when I think how much your growing fame has promifed to make you your parent's comfort and your fifter's friend, my heart mourns with anguifh on your danger."

The emotions which Lydia exhibited while fhe thus poured forth this forrowful ejaculation, deftroyed the fortitude which the Vicar had vainly imagined he had collected. The feelings of the parent, and, if it can with propriety be fo called, the weaknefs of the man, refumed the fulnefs of their power.

" 'Tis true, my child," he continued, " his virtues, as you fay, will render his lofs more intolerable; and if Francis dies, I feel my peace of mind is gone for ever. Forgive

Forgive me, Heaven! forgive a weak, infirm old man, who has too fondly built an edifice of hope, which, tottering to deftruction, threatens to invole in its demolition the fabric of his life!—My poor Francis, the darling of my departed angel!—Young as you were, Lydia, you muft remember the clofing period of her life, when furrounded by her weeping family, calm, mild, and compofed, fhe recommended you all to my care. While you ftood weeping at the foot of the bed, fhe called you to her. ' My little innocent,' faid fhe, ' be comforted, my Oufeley will be kind to my lambs:' and then refigned her foul into the hands of her Creator."

" Never," faid Lydia, " fhall I forget the icy preffure of her lips, or the clay-cold touch of her feeble hand."

" Glorious

"Glorious was her exit," replied the Vicar. "The tomb received her in the maturity of perfection, and her foul, fublimed and pure, fped on the wings of hope, faith, and immortality, to the manfions of the bleffed.—But oh, my fon! muft I lofe thee in the beginning of thy days? Indeed, my Lydia, I fear. he will part from us.— Can I ever bear the fight of that rafh, imprudent girl, whofe giddinefs has thus fatally expofed her name to be the fport of the licentious; whofe friends, family, reputation, all were facrificed to an infatiate thirft for admiration? Oh! no, no; fhe is unworthy of the name of child."

"Oh, fay not fo!" cried Lydia; "my fifter, in agonies, befeeches to fee you. On my knees I entreat that you will comply with her requeft. Oh, were you to fee her, pale and languifhing, her gentle nature fhocked ſhocked and terrified at the ſad event! you know, Sir, ſhe has not a vicious heart.— How often have you ſaid that humanity ſhould excuſe the venial faults of nature. You are not, Sir, of an inflexible diſpoſition. Come then, Sir, come to your child, ſooth her into comfort, and ſay that you forgive her."

The Vicar melted into tears at the pathetic exhortation of his daughter, and raiſing her to his arms—" You have conquered all my reſentment, Lydia," he cried. Poor Roſina! the beſt may err. Shall I not aid to recover the tranquillity of my child? One is already gone—oh no! Heaven may yet in its mercy reſtore him.'

With compaſſionate tenderneſs he aſcended the ſtairs to Roſina's room; who, upon hearing the footſteps of her father, ſunk almoſt fainting on the boſom of her

aunt,

aunt, crying, in great affliction, " Oh, he will not, he cannot forgive me!"

" Behold," said Miss Margaret, as he entered the room, " behold the situation of my lovely girl; and if your heart is not harder than a tiger's, you will afford her consolation."

" The human mind," said Mr. Ouseley as he advanced, " softened by affliction, forgets its resentments, and seeks, by offices of tenderness, to lessen the wretchedness of others, and to alleviate its own. Look up, my Rosina, nor aggravate my distress by your tears."

Rosina fell prostrate at his feet. He kindly raised her from the ground, and folded her in his arms. " Let us not," said he, " by murmurings and complaints, appear to arraign the ways of Heaven; without whose permission the rash hand of Melford could

not

not have ſtruck this blow at the darling of our hopes. Let us rather, like mutual ſufferers on a ſea of affliction, endeavour to ſave each other, and avoid a total wreck. Should the dire calamity we ſo much dread overtake us——" But nature made a pauſe, an awful pauſe; and he was unable to proceed.

The tenderneſs of her father revived the ſinking ſpirits of Roſina. She attended her aunt and her ſiſter to the room where her brother lay, who ſtill remained ſenſeleſs, and unable to ſpeak. The next morning, however, he uttered a few incoherent expreſſions, and at length recovered his faculties ſo far as to recollect his family.

The wound ſtill exhibited appearances extremely alarming; and the apothecary prognoſticated an increaſe of fever from ſymptoms which, he whiſpered Miſs Margaret

garet, had entirely deftroyed the few hopes he before entertained of his patient's re-covery.

The anguiſh which tore the boſom of Roſina when ſhe received this intelligence is beyond defcription.   Confcience upbraided her mind with the guilt of her conduct, and placed the poffible effects of it in the moſt horrid point of view.   The man whom her heart adored, miſguided in his conceptions of her character from the levity of her be-haviour, had given this ſtab to the happi-neſs of her family.   The image of a lover imbruing his hands in the vital blood of a beloved brother, haunted her inceffantly like a frightful ſpectre.   Her own reflections increaſed the pang of every ſorrow, and pierced her feelings with an envenomed dart.

Suſpenſe,

Sufpenfe, the moft painful paffion of the foul, tortured the minds of this anxious family for feveral days; and, as the fever was now faft approaching to its crifis, attended with fymptoms of the moft malignant nature, no hopes remained. Francis, whofe life promifed diffufive felicity to his connections, now appeared haftening to the cold manfions of the dead, where the wicked can betray no more, the weary are at reft, and the good find immortal happinefs and calm repofe.

CHAP.

CHAP. XVII.

THE RETURN OF PEACE.

THE nerves of Francis were ftrung with youth; and the inveteracy of his difeafe ftrove in vain againft the ftrength of nature. We fhall not, therefore, have occafion to detain our readers long in the chamber of an invalid. Hygeia, the blooming Goddefs of Health, again returned to reanimate his veins, to re-illumine his eyes with their wonted fire, and promifed, in proper time, to repaint his cheeks with her unrivalled rouge.

The neceffary confinement to his room was rendered lefs irkfome to him by the anxiety of his fifters to divert his mind; they read, fung, played, and chatted to him whenever his fpirits were able to bear the pleafures of fociety. The entertainment of reading, indeed, was generally under-taken by Mifs Margaret, who prided herfelf extremely upon her fuperior excellence in this elegant art, and fhe was highly delighted with the fondnefs which her nephew pro-feffed for the Novels which fhe read to him. The Vicar alfo contributed his fhare of en-tertainment, and promifed his fon much plea-fure from the reading of a treatife, which he had written upon the fubject of the cardinal virtues. Poor Francis, however, happened

to

to doze a little in the moſt intereſting part of the work, and the Vicar was not a little diſconcerted by his inattention; but it afforded ſingular triumph to Miſs Margaret, as he had liſtened very attentively to a long hiſtory which ſhe had read to him the preceding evening.

Health is much eaſier deſtroyed than reſtored, and although the ſtrength of our patient's conſtitution had baffled the fever in its moſt furious attack, and placed danger at a conſiderable diſtance, yet his ſtrength returned by very ſlow degrees; he was, however, ſo much recovered as to introduce a converſation upon the occaſion of his illneſs.

The Vicar remonſtrated with great ſeriouſneſs againſt the intemperance of a paſſion which could lead to an action ſo raſh, ſo cruel, ſo derogatory to the firſt principles

of

of benevolence and humanity—an action
which carried the appearance of an attempt
to rush uncalled and prematurely into the
prefence of the Almighty—an action repugnant to the facred injunction which commands us " not to let the fun go down
upon our wrath."

Francis, with the candour and generofity
of his nature, acknowledged the error of
which he had been guilty, and exculpated
Captain Melford from all blame. He confeffed the propriety of his father's fentiments
upon the fubject, and liftened with patience,
conviction, and gratitude to his words.

Rofina's mind, now relieved from all apprehenfion of her brother's death, or her
lover's danger, thought no more of thofe
long trains of ills which had before tortured
her fancy. The ruffet robes of Griffet, and
Queen Efther's garment of fackcloth and
                                        afhes,

aſhes, vaniſhed from her mind; and ſhe received a very ſevere rebuke from Lydia for ſuffering ſome gruel, which ſhe had undertaken to make for her brother, to boil over into the fire, while ſhe was trying on a new cap at the glaſs, to ſee how it would ſuit the preſent delicacy of her complexion. Lydia aſked her, a little peeviſhly, if it was for the pleaſure only of looking in the glaſs that ſhe was dreſſing, but recollecting that young Sedgeley had been invited to ſpend the evening with Francis, another motive immediately ſuggeſted itſelf to her mind, as ſhe knew her ſiſter's deſire to keep all her admirers within her trammels.

In proportion as the health of Francis returned, happineſs was reſtored to the family, the bright beams of peace once more ſhed their enlivening influence upon the Vicar's houſe, and joy and felicity returned

to

to that abode, where, foftered by innocence, they had fo long flourifhed.

> " In Nature's faireft forms, is aught fo fair
> " As virtuous friendfhip? is the candid blufh
> " Of him who ftrives with fortune to be juft?
> " The graceful tear that ftreams for others' woes?
> " Or the mild majefty of private life,
> " Where peace with ever-blooming olive crowns
> " The gate, when Honour's liberal hands effufe
> " Unenvied treafures, and the fnowy wings
> " Of Innocence and Love protect the fcene?"

THE PLEASURES OF IMAGINATION.

END OF VOL. I.

4 DE 58

Lightning Source UK Ltd.
Milton Keynes UK
UKOW06f1931041113

220438UK00015B/970/P